W9-CJI-221

RELIGION IN PLATO AND CICERO

RELIGION
IN PLATO AND CICERO

By JOHN E. REXINE

GREENWOOD PRESS, PUBLISHERS
NEW YORK   1968

Upsala College
Library
East Orange, N. J. 07019

184
C
R 455n

© Copyright, 1959, by
Philosophical Library, Inc.
Reprinted with the permission of the Philosophical Library, Inc.

First Greenwood reprinting, 1968

LIBRARY OF CONGRESS catalogue card number: 68-28581

Printed in the United States of America

153204

IN MEMORIAM

MEAE MATRIS CARISSIMAE ATHENAE

TABLE OF CONTENTS

PREFACE

This study was originally written at the suggestion of Professor Arthur Darby Nock of Harvard University, to whose acute criticism and helpful guidance the author is deeply indebted and whose remarkable teaching and scholarship have always been a source of inspiration to his students and colleagues. The chapter on "Plato's Attitude toward the Poets in the *Laws*" owes much to the inspiration of Professor William Chase Greene of Harvard University, from whom I have learned more about Platonic Greek than from any other source perhaps than Plato himself. Both these scholars, who were teachers of mine at Harvard University, deserve recognition for bringing out any merits this study may have. Any *vitia* are purely of my own making.

The *Laws* of Plato are frequently referred to but very infrequently read or studied. One can say with even more assurance that the *Laws* of Cicero are even less known than the *Laws* of Plato. It has been my intention in this study to concentrate on the role of religion in a general comparative study of these two great representatives of the Greek and Roman worlds, to show the essential part played by religion in both the *Laws* of Plato and those of Cicero, and to demonstrate by a comparison of the respective texts wherein lie the principal differences and similarities in the views of these two men on a universally interesting and important subject. To isolate religion from other topics is, of course, an artificial modern process and tends to violate the assumption that the classical man was the "whole man," at least much more of a whole man than modern man is. However, the author feels that this study, which concentrates on specific references from the texts concerned, serves the purpose

1

of concentrating much needed light on the role that religion played in the theories of Plato and Cicero in the *Laws* of both men, and perhaps more useful for many, that this light helps us to understand better Platonic and Ciceronian ideas that are basic to their respective philosophies as a whole. For a masterful study of Plato's theology the reader is urged to refer to Friedrich Solmsen's *Plato's Theology* (Ithaca: Cornell University Press, 1942) in the series *Cornell Studies in Classical Philology*, Vol. XXVII.

This study is essentially a study of a Greek and a Latin text. Unfortunately, the author has seen the necessity for employing English translations of the Greek of Plato and transliterations to enable the general Greekless reader to profit from the book.

In arriving at my sometimes all too literal translations of the Plato, I have used the Greek text of E. B. England, *The Laws of Plato* in two volumes (Manchester: At the University Press, 1921), Caroli Friderici Hermanni, *Platonis Dialogi secundum Thrasylli Tetralogias Dispositi, Vol. V* (B. G. Teubner: Leipzig, 1852), and John Burnet, *Platonis Opera*, Vol. V (Oxford: At the Clarendon Press, 1952), as well as consulted the translations of Benjamin Jowett, *The Dialogues of Plato Translated into English*, With an Introduction by Professor Raphael Demos, in two volumes (New York: Random House, 1937), vol. 2, pp. 407-703 and the Loeb Library text and translation of R. G. Bury, *Plato: Laws* in two volumes (Cambridge, Mass. and London: Harvard University Press and William Heineman Ltd., 1952). A. E. Taylor's *The Laws of Plato* (London, 1934) has been indispensable throughout this study. Other acknowledgments are duly credited in the notes. All the books mentioned above have been very useful for this study and the interested reader is referred to them for detailed examination. For Cicero's *Laws* the most convenient text is the Loeb Library edition by Clinton Walker Keyes (Cicero: *De Re Publica* and *De Legibus*).

I must thank my colleague, Professor Robert L. Murray of Colgate University, for consenting to go through the arduous process of reading the entire proof and Mr. Leigh Winser of Colgate for checking the Greek passages and helping with sundry other matters in the preparation of this manuscript, as

2

well as my wife Elaine, whose patience and understanding as well as criticism have been very useful. To Professor J. Curtiss Austin, Chairman of the Department of Classics at Colgate University, I should like to acknowledge publicly that I have learned many things from him in stimulating private conversations about the classical world that I have oftentimes missed in publications or never learned in formal courses. To the staff of the Philosophical Library, I owe cordial thanks for their interest in this humble work, their patience in seeing to its publication, and their technical assistance and expertness.

Colgate University   JOHN E. REXINE
Hamilton, N. Y.

A COMPARATIVE STUDY OF RELIGION IN
PLATO'S *LAWS* AND CICERO'S *LAWS*

I

General Introduction

This essay purports to study the subject of religion on the basis of references to this subject in Plato's *Laws* and in Cicero's *Laws* and to indicate the similarities and differences that may exist between the views of a great Greek philosopher and those of the great orator of Rome. It further purports to point out wherein Cicero's views and statements concerning religion in his *Laws* actually reflect Roman practice and whether Cicero has anything original, anything of his own to offer to the subject of religion in his *Laws*. This essay will involve a close reading of the passages in Plato's *Laws* and Cicero's *Laws* which have to do with the subject of religion and only occasional references to other works will be cited. Plato's *Laws*, in a very real sense, presupposes Plato's *Republic* and Cicero's *Laws* presupposes Cicero's *De Re Publica*. However, it is not the purpose of this essay to examine such relationships. The *Laws* of Plato are not the laws of Plato's *Republic* by any means. On the other hand, it is quite clear that Cicero's *Laws* are the laws of Cicero's *De Re Publica*.[1] This essay, in no way, purports to be exhaustive, but rather suggestive. The subject of religion, in all its aspects, including theology, will be outlined as taken from the two authors with whom this paper is concerned, but only their discussion of religion as it appears in their respective *Laws* will be cited.

II

Religion in Plato's *Laws*

It is perhaps easy to surmise, even by those who know something of Plato and Cicero, but who have not read their respective *Laws,* that even in the subject of religion Plato would have some original thoughts on the matter along with a good many traditionally Greek statements, and that Cicero would be perhaps inclined to be a traditionalist in the matter, even though strict adherence to the traditional Roman religious practice may not have been an actuality in his day. These points our study of the texts involved will surely bring out.

A mere glance at the texts involved will show that Plato's *Laws* is almost completely preserved in twelve books whereas Cicero's is badly preserved and mutilated with only three books preserved (for the most part) and a very small fragment from the Fifth Book. There were at least five books in the original. There probably were six books, but even eight have been suggested.[2] The *Laws* of Plato is a sort of compromise on the *Republic* of Plato. We might describe it as a description of the best possible state under the practical conditions then existent, whereas the ideal state of the *Republic* is described in these terms:

> "Well," I said, "perhaps there is a pattern laid up in heaven for the man who is willing to see and seeing, to establish a city in himself. It makes no difference whether it exists somewhere or will exist. For whatever he should do would be characteristic of this city alone; it would be characteristic of no other." [3]

6

However, our concern at present is the subject of religion, and it would perhaps be wisest for us to plunge into our subject *hôs táchista* and not be enticed from our subject by other no less fascinating subjects that are prominent in the texts under discussion.

Let us then begin with the *Laws of Plato.*

References to religion are not confined to any one book (though Book X concerns itself almost exclusively with Platonic theology), but are scattered throughout the work. In order to provide some order to our discussion, it will perhaps be profitable to discuss Plato's views topically.

What are the religious duties of the individual citizens in Plato's *Laws?* What is to be the citizen's mode of religious behavior? How is he to act with respect to the Theos? What are the consequences of such behavior as prescribed by Plato? Or what happens if such behavior is not in accordance with the prescribed behavior? In short, what are the religious duties of the citizen to be and why? Plato answers us in Book IV of the *Laws.* The Athenian speaks.[4]

"Well, then, gentlemen," we say to them, "God, therefore, as the ancient saying goes, holding the beginning, the end, and the middle of all things that are and proceeding according to his nature in a straight line brings his business to accomplishment. Justice always accompanies him and is the punisher of those who desert the divine law, to which, on the one hand, he would be fortunate to cling who is humble and ordered but, on the other hand, he who is exalted by arrogance or money, and excited either by honors and the beauty of flesh also, at the same time through youth and want or understanding is ablaze in his soul with insolence, thinking that he has no god, *he* is left behind; and having been thus forsaken and adding still other such men also, leaps about throwing everything into confusion at the same time, and to many he seemed to be reputable and after a short while, suffering the penalty which receives the approbation of justice, he utterly ruined himself, his household and his city. With respect to these things, therefore, that have been thus ordered, what should a prudent man do or think or not do or think?" [5]

In the passage quoted above Plato clearly answers certain questions. God exists and, in accordance with tradition, holds the beginning, the end, and the middle of all existing things. The path that God follows is unswerving and orderly, and along with him comes Justice (Díkê) as an avenger (timôrós) of those people who fall short of the Divine Law (toû theíou nómou). Whoever is wise will see to it that he complies with the requirements of Justice, for Justice is of God. Plato here exhorts the individual citizen to realize the Divine Essence and the divine origin of Justice. Through the words of the Athenian, he goes on to explain: "What line of action and thought should the prudent man pursue and what should he not?" The citizen has a right to know and must know what is required of him in his relationship with the Divine.

Clinias answers succinctly:

"It is accordingly obvious at any rate that every man must make up his mind that he will be one of those who will follow the god." [6]

It next remains to examine what line of human behavior toward the divine is to be followed. "What action then is dear to and in conformity with the god?" [7] A discussion follows in which the first point brought out refers back to the Homeric "God always brings like to like." [8] God will be the measure of all things "For us god, therefore, would particularly be the measure of all things." It will, therefore, become necessary for man to strive to become as much as possible of a similar character. "The prudent man, on the one hand, is dear to god, for he is like him; but on the other hand, he who is not prudent is both unlike him and different and unjust." The argument goes on to relate that to engage in sacrifices and communion with the gods continually by prayers and offerings and devotions of every kind is a thing most noble and good and helpful towards the happy life, and most excellently appropriate also for the good man, whereas the very opposite is true for the wicked:

"for the good man to offer sacrifice and to be constantly associating with the gods by means of prayers and offerings and every sort of service to the gods is the finest and best and most effectual for a happy life and particularly fitting, but for the bad man the opposite naturally holds true."

Plato emphasizes a point here that has to do with the validity of religious function of an impure as opposed to a pure man. The religious functions of a pure man are religiously valid, but those of an impious, those of a wicked man, are not:

"For the bad man surely possesses a filthy soul, while the good man has a pure soul. It is surely impossible for either a good man or a god to accept gifts from an impure person. In vain therefore do the impure ones expend much effort on the gods but the efforts of pure persons are always seasonable."

It pays to be pious, Plato informs us, for not even a good man can rightly accept a gift from one that is defiled in religious terms, let alone a god. All should aim at achieving this piety ("Such is the target at which we should all aim.").

It would be interesting for the reader at this point to keep in mind a really contrasting view of Cicero's who pleads, in several passages of the *Laws* for the divine kinship of man with gods. Cicero will tell us that all human souls are mortal, but that the soul of a good man is divine.

Then follows an obscure passage on the order of worship to be paid to the gods. After due worship has been paid to the Olympians and the patron deities of the State ("[We assert] that after the Olympian deities and the gods of the city honor should be rendered the chthonians"), the even and the left should be assigned to the gods of the underworld "to the chthonian deities ..."

9

The explanation is apparently based on the Pythagorean doctrine of the opposites. The odd number is superior to the even, and the right side to the left. It is here stated that honors of a superior kind are to be offered up to the Olympian gods or to the patron deities of the State, whereas secondary honors go to the chthonian deities. After due honors have been paid to the Olympian deities and patron gods of the State, and to the chthonic deities, worship should be offered "to the *numina* and after them to the heroes. . . ." [9]

After the daemons and the heroes, it will be the duty of the good and wise citizen to tend to private shrines legally dedicated "with the ritual celebrated according to law," and to honors to be paid to his living parents. Of legally dedicated shrines Plato will speak again in no uncertain terms.[10]

The proper respect due parents both living and dead, is the next subject with which Plato is occupied. Just as a debtor should repay his greatest debts first, so it is meet for man to discharge his most outstanding debt, debt to his parents. The words of Plato are very human and touching on this point:

> ". . . he believes that all which a man has got and possesses are all the property of those who have given him birth and reared him and that he must do everything possible in their service; beginning first with his property; second, with his body; third, with his soul paying back what he has borrowed in terms of care and the old pains which they suffered for him when he was an infant and returning these in their old age when they need them most . . ." [11]

Respect for parents, especially in tongue, is stressed:

> "since for all, Nemesis, the messenger of Justice, has been appointed to watch over such matters." [12]

On the occasion of the parent's death, proper funeral rites must be observed. Funeral expenses should not be lavish and excessive. Propriety should be observed. Rites should be strictly administered in accordance with available means, but with no

10

excessive display. Plato advises us to do these things because they will result in rewards from the gods:

> "By doing this and living our lives in accordance with these terms each one of us will receive his due reward from the gods and from as many as are better than we are, passing the largest part of our life in good expectations." [13]

With respect to duties toward children, relations, friends, and citizens, as well as service done to strangers for the sake of the gods and relations with the lot of them, Plato informs us that the Law will take care that proper legislative action is taken and administered.

A. E. Taylor, in his preface to his translation of Plato's *Laws,* provides an admirable summary of the religious functions of the citizen:[14]

> "God eternally pursues the even tenour of his way, and Justice is God's attendant. To be happy a man must follow Justice and God with a 'humbled and disciplined soul,' and to 'follow' God means to be like God, who—and not man, as Protagoras has said—is the true 'measure' of everything. To be like God, then, is to lead the life of right 'measure,' and the first principle of this life is to have a true scale of moral worth. Reverence, or honour, is to be paid to its recipients in their proper order, and the proper order is to give the first place to the gods of the world of the living and the patron deities of the city, the second to the gods of the dim world beyond the grave, the third to 'daemons and heroes'—or as a Christian might say to 'angels' and the canonized saints—the fourth to departed ancestors in general, the fifth to our still living parents, and only the sixth to ourselves and the men of our own generation."

The reader will not find such precise instructions on the proper worship procedures in the *De Legibus* of Cicero. Plato is very explicit when it comes to religion. He sets down the pattern for belief just as he sets down the pattern for the ideal state. Cicero will take a great many of the religious ideas that he wants observed for granted. The reader is expected to fill in the details from actual Roman practice. Cicero, we shall see in his own words, has a profound respect for Roman religious tradition.

We now come to Plato's discussion of religious foundations, temples, shrines, festivals, and related matters. In the matter of temples, Plato expresses a view that may be briefly described as traditionalist and conservative. The lawgiver should in no way attempt to alter the traditional gods, shrines, and temples which have been established. No legislator should be so foolish as to attempt to go against advice that has its origin in Delphi, Dodona or Ammon. To each section of the city, it should be the charge of the Nomothétês to see to it that a god, daemon, or at least a hero is assigned. The Nomothétês should even distribute the land and assign to these select domains gods with all the appropriate trappings. Such an arrangement would have a unifying effect in that the people could get together on religious occasions and mutual friendliness could be cultivated with fitting, beneficial results for all parties concerned.[15]

Again in Book VIII,[16] in his *Stadtplan,* Plato deals with the setting up of temples. Plato also shows that due respect must be paid to the shrines of ancient local deities of the Magnetes or any other shrines of other ancient gods whose memory is still revered. We shall see that in this respect for ancient ancestral gods Cicero is in complete agreement with Plato. "First then in each village a market place and temples of the gods and the *numina* who accompany them will be set aside." Temples to Hestia, Zeus, and Athena are to be erected everywhere, as well as to any other divinity ". . . and to whatever (god) may be presiding officer in each of the twelve parts . . ." Buildings are to be set up round these temples on the highest ground possible to provide the strongest vantage point for the garrison. We shall find that Plato repeats this point in another passage later.

In Book XII,[17] we are told that "The man of moderation should make modest offerings to the gods." We shall find this theme of "proper measure" expressed also by Cicero when it comes to religious dedications. "The land . . . and the hearth of dwelling" are sacred to all the gods. No rededication is therefore permissible for what has already been duly dedicated. Gold, silver, and ivory are not considered objects of valid religious dedication. Gold and silver cause jealousy and envy; ivory is unclean, impure because it comes from a dead body. Neither are bronze nor iron objects proper for dedicatory purpose because of their connection with war. Plato suggests instead, that if a pious person desires to make a proper offering, he may do so with something of wood or stone or a piece of woven work which one woman can complete in not more than a month. The most suitable of colors for dedicatory purposes is white—the eternal symbol of purity. Dyes are not appropriate except for military decorations. The most pious gifts are birds and statues, and these should not exceed in size what one sculptor can produce in one day "lest other offerings also be represented in like fashion." All the preceding, we shall find Cicero repeating in Book II of his *Laws,* though it is not fair to assume that Cicero went along completely with all these Platonic proposals. Cicero would agree with the Platonic plea for moderation in these matters, but he certainly would not go as far as Plato does. Another point which it is perhaps important to point out here is that there seems to be a decided connection between these limitations that Plato would set on religious offerings and his bitter condemnation of those who would attempt to bribe the gods with lavish gifts. Book X contains a vivid account of the "heresy" of believing in the doctrine that it is possible for an impious man to win the gods over with gifts.

In Book VI,[18] we have an echo of a passage already cited above from Book V (738B2-E8): "So we must trust in our present task to the traditional belief in question and make this division. Each section will be called by the name of a god or a child of the gods and provided with altars and their furniture, where we shall convoke two sacrificial assemblies per month—twelve for the divisions into tribes and twelve for the corresponding section of the town itself; their first purpose will be to ensure the divine favor and to promote religion, and their second, from our point of view, to encourage mutual intimate acquaintances and social intercourse of all kinds."

As for private shrines, Plato is explicitly clear. It would not do to have such a thing in a Platonic state. Worship is encouraged, but worship is to be performed at the public temples. It is the business of the priests to consecrate. It is even better if the citizens worship together with others who may be of their own choosing. Cicero will point out similar things in his *Laws,* Book II. The priests are there to do a certain job he will tell us. New gods or foreign gods will tend to vitiate the functions of the native priests and will bring confusion into the established religion, not to mention certain other subversive tendencies that private worship, especially of new or foreign gods, would bring in. But, here are Plato's comments:

> "Let no one have sacred rites in a private house; but when anyone wants to offer sacrifice let him proceed to make his sacrificial offering publicly and let him entrust his offerings to both priests and priestesses who are charged with the strict observance of religious duties. Let him pray himself and let anyone who wishes join him in prayer. Let these things be done this way for the following reasons: it is not an easy thing to establish temples and gods; and to have the vision to see such a thing as this through rightly is the mark of a great mind." [19]

There has been too great a lack of careful and tasteful discrimination, says Plato, in the dedication of temples. Therefore, such action must be governed by law. The implication is also strong that private worship and privately dedicated temples or shrines are invitations to "heresy." Public control of worship, Plato seems to say, will ensure the maintenance of the established religion and will provide stability for the state. No doubt, a staunch Roman *pater* would agree most heartily with the foregoing statement. Plato will not compromise. Impious men, wicked men, will not be permitted to attempt propitiation of the gods by setting up private hierá. For this shall be the law:

> "No man shall have gods' shrines in a private home and whoever has been revealed to possess one and performs

rites other than public ones, if the man or woman who has been caught has not committed any great impieties, let him who knows lay the information before the guardians. The guardians will then issue orders for him to remove his private rites to the public temples and if they do not obey, let them be penalized until they are removed. And if a person is obviously guilty of impiety not from childish affront but from adult impiety, whether he has sacrificed to any of the gods whatsoever publicly or privately, let him be penalized with the death penalty as being impure and as not performing sacrifice. Let the guardians of the law judge whether he has acted through childishness or not before bringing him thus into court for prosecution on charges of impiety." [20]

Plato is very serious about this matter. Only by being so stringent as he proposes can society be kept from falling into the "error of wrong belief."

There are several other passages that should perhaps be cited for a fair amount of completeness under this subdivision. In Book V, we find a dividing up of the city into twelve parts corresponding to the twelve Olympian deities. First, the lawgiver should establish and enclose sanctuaries of Hestia, Zeus, and Athena. To this he will give the name *akrópolis* and surround it with a *kýklos*. Later on, in this same passage, twelve portions are administratively divided:

"After this they shall assign twelve lots to the twelve gods and call them by their names, and consecrate each allotted portion to the god concerned and name the tribes after him." [21]

The sanctuary is not merely important religiously, but it is, highly respected and is considered definitely so sacred that Plato would have elections held in the most highly esteemed shrine in the state.

"And the election shall take place in a temple which the city state considers the most honorable and each person will

15

carry this ballot to the altar of the god, having written the name of his father, of his tribe and deme in which he is enrolled, on the tablet and at the side of the same tablet he will inscribe his own name in a similar fashion." [22]

Book VI contains a passage which repeats certain of the information that we saw above.[23] The temples are to be erected round the market place and in a circle round the whole city on the highest sites with a view at once to security and cleanliness:

"The temples therefore are to be built around the market place and the entire city constructed in a circle on the heights for the sake of both security and cleanliness." [24]

Above we cited the fact that Plato would utilize the most highly esteemed temple for the purpose of elections. In Book XII, we discover that tourists are to be provided for by the priests and sacristans who will provide them with lodgings at the local temples. Any wrong undergone by the tourists under the amount of fifty drachmas will be settled by the priests; anything above that stated amount will be referred to the Commissioners of the Market for proper adjudication.[25] Imagine the effect on modern tourism if it were placed in the charge of the priests and the church! Paris would never be the same if Plato got control!

Deputations to the various oracles, games, and sacrifices, are all provided for. Plato is all in favor of deputations to Apollo of Pytho, Zeus of Olympia, as well as to Nemea and to the Isthmus. Plato emphasizes that those who are sent to such places to participate in the sacrifices and games honoring the gods should be as many, as noble, and as outstanding as possible. Those who are sent on such religious mission should be such as will render the *pólis* glorious in religious and peace congresses, and bestow upon it a glory commensurate with her repute in the battlefield.[26]

At this point in our discussion, it would perhaps be wise to indicate that Plato began to outline the religious needs of the state in Book VI. Plato informs us quite lucidly that there will

16

have to be a priesthood—sacristans, priests, and priestesses for the temples. In the administration of the state there will have to be priests and priestesses. Any priests or priestesses whose dignity is hereditary have to be left alone. Where there is need, priests should be instituted. The priests will be selected by a joint process of lot and election, though a close scrutiny of the candidate's character and background will be made:

"Accordingly, the men in charge of the temples shall be chosen according to lot. Thus their election will be due to divine providence. He who wins a position shall subject himself constantly to investigation as to whether he is whole and legitimate. Thereupon, he must demonstrate that he is from the purest possible family background, free from guilt in murder and all other such crimes, and also that both his father and mother have lived undefiled lives."

Plato proceeds to tell us that they ought to bring laws about all matters of religion from Delphi: ". . . laws concerning all divine matter should be conveyed from Delphi." Appointments for interpreters will have to be made. The tenure of each priestly office is to be for one year only. The person officiating in a priestly capacity should have attained at least the age of sixty. The exêgêtaí will be elected. These men will have life tenure. The twelve tribes will be divided into three groups of four each. Each group will appoint three, making nine exêgêtaí in all. The remaining three needed to complete the full twelve will be selected by the oracle from a list of nine candidates who are next in order. Treasurers (tamíai) in charge of the sacred moneys in each of the temples and the precincts and their produce along with their rents must be selected from the highest property classes. Three men will be assigned to the largest temples, two for the smaller, and one for the least extensive. The same method will be utilized for the selection and examination of the treasurers.[27]

The religious calendar and the religious festivals are by no means neglected by Plato in his remarks on religion. From Book VIII, we learn:

"Then with the assistance of the oracle at Delphi, holidays have to be established and laws made relating to them. In addition, it must be determined what sacrificial offerings should be made and to what gods it would be rather good and beneficial that they would be offered. It would be partly our responsibility to legislate when and how often the offerings should be made."

The number of feast days is set at at least 36. This is done in order that sacrifice to some god or spirit (*daímôn*) in behalf of the State, the people, and their possessions will always be transpiring. *Exêgêtai*, priests, and priestesses, and the soothsayers are to meet in conjunction with the *Nomophýlakes* and determine what the *Nomothétês* will be compelled to omit. The law will provide for twelve feasts to the twelve gods from whom the twelve tribes shall derive their respective names. The law will also provide for sacrifices, choruses, musical contests, and women's festivals:

"The law will declare that there are twelve feast days consecrated to the twelve gods after whom each tribe is named; and that to each of them they sacrifice each month and arrange for choruses and musical contests as well as gymnastic competitions fittingly correspondent with the several gods and at the same time with each of the several seasons also. And they shall have women's feast days, separating those which ought to be set off from the feast days, of men and those which ought not to be set off. Furthermore, not confusion but a distinction must be made between chthonic divinities and these who are called heavenly and their rites. In the twelfth month they must give to Pluto his own rites in his own month in accordance with the law. Even pugnacious men must not feel dislike at this god, but must honor him as always being the best friend of the human race." [28]

Provision is also made for noble games with prizes for the winning contestants. These games are to take place along with the sacrifices. There will also be speeches of praise (*enkômia*):

"And they should always devise noble games along with sacrifices in order to become festival tournaments, imitating in as vivid a fashion as possible actual battles. At each of these they must award prizes of victory and bravery and make encomiastic or censorious speeches for one another depending on the characters which they reflect in the contests and in their entire life, embellishing him who seems to be best and reproaching him who is not." [29]

In Book II, Plato tells us why the gods have provided religious festivals for man. The festivals were the result of divine compassion for man's miserable condition. The gods in their kindness wanted to grant man relief from this hardship at stated periods and also grant companions to the feasts in the persons of the Muses, Apollo, and Dionysos:

"And the gods, taking pity on mankind which is destined to suffer toil, have established feast days of thanksgiving as rest from their toils and have given them the Muses and Apollo the leader of the Muses and Dionysus as fellow companions in the feast in order that they might at least correct again their education through their companionship with the gods in the feast." [30]

From Book VII, we learn more about the religious festivals and Plato's unswerving attitude toward the poets:

"First, the festivals must be fixed by compiling an annual calendar to show what feasts are to be celebrated, at what dates, and in honor of what deities, sons of deities, or spirits respectively; next, certain authorities must determine what hymn is to be sung on the feast day of each divinity and by what dances the ceremony of the day is to be graced; when this has been determined, the whole citizen body must do public sacrifice to the Destinies (*Moîra*) and the entire Pantheon at large, and consecrate each hymn to its respective god or other patron by solemn libation. If any man tries to introduce hymn or dance into the worship of any deity in contravention of these canons, the priests of either sex acting in conjunction with the Curators of Law (Nomophýlakes), shall have the warrant both of religion and the law in excluding him from the festival; if the excluded party declines to submit to this excommunication, he shall for life be liable to indictment for impiety at the instance of anyone who cares to institute proceedings." [31]

Plato has in his *Laws* an interesting note on the definition of a prayer. It is contained in his discussion of what the poets must do in order to make themselves acceptable to his *politeía* in the *Nómói*. Plato enlightens us thus:

"... that the poets, knowing that *prayers are requests made of the gods,* must accordingly pay very careful attention lest they unknowingly request an evil thing in place of a good thing. For surely this would be ridiculous, if a prayer like this were actually offered up." [32]

It will, of course, be most appropriate to sing hymns and praises to the gods accompanied with prayers. After the gods, due honors should go to the *daímones* and the heroes. We have seen this order explained early in our discussion:

"In the next place it would be absolutely correct to have hymns of the gods and doxologies of them commingled with prayers; and after the gods in the same fashion would prayers along with doxologies be offered to the *numina* and heroes—most fitting prayers for all these." [33]

As with dedications, Plato insists upon observation of strict moderation in the matter of funerals and funeral expenses. These sentiments, we shall see, are re-echoed by Cicero in his *Laws*. Plato even sets the maximum amount of verse that may appear on a funerary stone, as well as the amount of money that may be expended for burial ceremonies:

"And a mound of earth must not be piled higher than it would take five men to complete the task in five days. And they must not make the stone slabs which are placed over the spot larger than is needed to contain the dead man's epitaph in no more than four dactylic hexameters. And the laying out of the deceased must not take more time than is necessary to distinguish between one who is unconscious from one who is really dead. Therefore, under normal circumstances the third day after his demise will be a perfectly humane time for him to be conveyed to his final resting place." [34]

The examiners of the magistrates, Plato tells us, are to be religious men also. They are to have the front seats at every festival, and in the case of delegations sent out to participate in any public sacrifices, assemblies, or other such holy gatherings of the Greeks. These shall be greatly honored, both when living and dead. Plato goes into details as to the honors that these examiners will be entitled to:

"And these men alone or those in the city shall be decorated with the crown of laurel and they shall all be archpriests of both Apollo and Helios and one of them who is judged the first of those who became priests that year, will become the high priest and his name will be inscribed in every year so as to serve as the measure of chronology as long as the city is inhabited. And when they have passed away, their laying out, carrying out, and entombment will be different from the rest of the citizens. They will wear a completely white garment. There shall be no lamentations or wailings. There shall be a chorus of fifteen maidens and fifteen men standing around their bier on both sides and throughout the entire day they shall sing antiphonally in turn for the priests in the form of a versified hymn, blessing them with their song. And at dawn one hundred young men who participate in gymnastic activities, and whom the relatives of the deceased shall choose, shall carry the bier itself to the sepulchre. The young men shall march first, each of them dressed in military uniforms, the cavalry on horseback, the hoplites with their

21

UPSALA COLLEGE LIBRARY

weapons, and the others in similar fashion. And the young men around the bier and those in front of it shall sing the national anthem and the girls following behind them shall sing also. This group will include as many women as happen to be free of child-bearing. Next shall follow the priests and priestesses as if on their way to a purified sepulchre, even if they are barred from all other tombs, unless of course the Pythian oracle concurs in like manner in their debarment from this also. Their sepulchre shall be constructed under the earth—an oblong vault of porous stone and stones that will last as long as possible. These sepulchres shall have situated stone couches side by side. Here, therefore, they shall lay out the blessed one and piling up earth in a circle, they shall plant around it a grove of trees except on one side so that the sepulchre shall always have room for expansion should it require additional mounds for those laid to rest. And every year they shall hold musical, gymnastic, and horse-racing contests in their honor." [35]

The above passage was quoted at great length to illustrate the close interconnection that the religious administrator is to have with the political situation. In practice, no such division of political and religious spheres is really possible. In Plato, religion is essential in the overall plan. It is an integral part of the body politic. It might be described as the spinal cord of the body politic. It is needed for the stability of the state, and the men of religion are important men in the state administration. Note, for example, that in the Perpetual Council of Public Safety, which is to made up of three groups, the priests who have won distinctions of the first rank are first to be listed; then follow ten senior acting Curators, and finally the last elected Minister of Education and any of the retired holders of that office.[36] Roman practice, it must be admitted, ideally purported to maintain the religious forms, though politicians made good use of high priestly offices for certain very practical ends.

Religion for Plato in the Laws is a very serious matter. No

deviations are to be tolerated. Violation of sacred injunctions is to be severely dealt with. Witness, for example, that the death penalty is prescribed for temple robbers and sacrilege[37] (díkê dè toútôi thánatos eláchiston tôn kakôn). We shall notice later on that Cicero is by no means that explicit about this matter.

III

The Theology of Book X of Plato's *Laws*

Thus far we have collected information in Plato's *Laws* which we might describe as pertaining to the practical exercise and function of religion. A good deal we have seen does not attempt to deviate from standard Greek religious practice. A good deal follows the traditional Greek pattern of the Greek cultic religion, though it must be admitted that Plato has exhibited a considerable number of Platonic ideas in connection with these religious practices, and what should be done to those who have violated the established religion or have deviated from it. "Plato could become the author of the proposal to 'persecute' for opinions precisely because he held that there are certain beliefs which are poisonous to the moral life of society, and that these beliefs can be proved to be false."[38]

We now come to a part of the Platonic religion in the *Laws* which is basic to the whole structure of the *Nómoi*. It is not merely important for the sake of inclusiveness in our discussion of religion in Plato's *Laws*, but it forms a significant starting-point for later theologians. It is Plato's theology to which almost the whole of Book X of the *Nómoi* is devoted. Book X ". . . is the foundation of all subsequent 'natural' theology, the first attempt in the literature of the world to *demonstrate* God's existence and moral government from the known facts of the visible order. First proposal . . . . to treat erroneous beliefs about God and the unseen world as crimes, and to erect an inquisition to suppress 'heretical pravity.' At Athens, as in other ancient

24

societies, 'impiety,' that is over-disrespect to the established *cultus* was, of course, a serious offence, but it seems clear that no mere expression about such matters was regarded as criminal."[39]

In Book XI, there is a single statement that would bear upon the theology of Book X and that could perhaps serve as an introductory statement to the more technical arguments from Book X to be outlined below. In Book XI, Plato informs us that:

> "The ancient laws concerning the gods are universally of two categories: for some of the gods we see clearly and we honor them; of others we set up their statues to which we pay honor as images, believing that although these images are lifeless, the living gods are on account of this very favorably disposed toward us and grateful to us."[40]

Such, says Plato, is the universal belief concerning the gods and their power. Believing in gods is nothing new with Plato. Plato is uncompromising with disbelievers. There is nothing comparable to it in Cicero's *De Legibus*, nor does Cicero's *Laws* contain such a powerful *tour de force* as Plato's proof for the existence of God.

Plato lucidly lists the three types of "heresies." They are as follows: (1) simple atheism: the denial that there are gods of any kind; (2) the doctrine that there are gods, but that they are completely unconcerned with or indifferent to human behavior and humanity; (3) the belief that there are gods who judge man, but that it is possible for the contrite offender to avoid the divine vengeance by bribing the gods with prayers and sacrifices. Why, it is even thought possible that a wicked man can do this and get away with it. Plato's bitter attack states that it is preferable to believe in no gods at all than to hold the belief that there are gods who are not concerned with man and his behavior; and that it is preferable to believe in gods that are not concerned with human behavior and man than to believe that gods exist and can be bribed or corrupted. Yet, in the final analysis, Plato would severely punish all three heretical groups.

It will now be up to the Nomothétès to set people straight about believing in gods and God. Too many have been misled.

25

The first point that Plato makes for the existence of God is based on universal custom and the cosmic order:

"In the first place there is the evidence of the earth and the sun and the stars and the entire universe and the beautiful order of the seasons, and their separation into both years and months. And then there is the fact that both all the Greeks and non-Greeks believe that the gods exist."[41]

The sun, moon, stars, and earth are called instances of divinity and deity:

"When we try to prove that the gods exist by offering in evidence these objects, namely, the sun and the moon and the stars and the earth as being gods or divine beings. . . ."[42]

This is not original with Plato, but is pointed out by him as being one of the ancient arguments used for proving the existence of divinities until it was subverted by the corporealism of the early Ionian scientists.

The next point that Plato makes is that, though one may hold non-belief in the gods in one's youth, he knows of no one who persisted in such "error" in old age, even though there are people who belong to the last two heretical categories listed above.[43]

Plato discusses the views of other thinkers on the nature of the universe, which we shall forbear from repeating here. Plato's real argument begins with the anteriority of the soul. All bodies involve motion or inertia.[44] All bodies are in motion or at rest, used to say the old physics books of our era. Motion or process (kínêsis) is of two types: (1) motion which is capable of moving other things but is not capable of moving itself (hê mén hetéra dyaménê kineîn kínêsis, heautên dè adynatoûsa) (2) motion which is always capable of moving itself and capable also of moving others (aeì mía tis, hê dè heautên t'aei kaì hétera dynaménê). One kind of motion may be called "imparted" or communicated" motion; the other "self-originated" motion. The first type of motion may also be described as secondary causation, and the second as primary causation. Plato goes on to show that primary causation is obviously first, prior in point of time and quality to all other kinds of motion:

> "Then we must necessarily assert that self-motion is the beginning of all motions and that it is the first to arise in things that are at rest and exist in things that are in motion and that it is the oldest and most powerful change of all, whereas the motion that moves other things is secondary in importance."[45]

The next step is that self-moving motion is indicative of a *psychê,* of something *émpsychon.* This step is inevitable. Any object that has the power to move itself as well as other objects contains a *psychê.* Before proceeding further with the argument, an observation about the properties of objects is made:

> "I mean that substance (essence) is one thing, that definition of the substance is one thing, and the name of substance is one thing." [46]

The word (*ónoma*)[47] Plato is interested in defining is *psychê* which is defined as a certain kind of motion:

> "The motion capable of moving itself. Do you mean to say that the motion that moves itself is the substance which we accordingly all call by the name of soul?"[48]

Thus we come to the thesis that soul=self-motion or primary causation. And so, our argument is firmly established along with the priority of the soul. It follows, then, that if the soul is prior to the body, moods, dispositions, wishes, calculations, true opinions, considerations, and memories are all prior to and sources of all the mechanical motions of the body, none of which are capable of self-starting.

It will therefore follow that the soul is the cause of all things, good and bad, fair and foul, just and unjust, and of all the opposites, if we grant the assumption that the soul is the *Ursache* of all things.[49] Of course, there will have to be more than one soul. In fact, there will have to be at least two souls; a good soul and a contrary or bad soul.

> "At any rate let us posit no less than two, i.e., the beneficent soul and the soul which is capable of working just the opposite effects."[50]

There may be as many souls as are needed to explain the actual situation. In the world, we can readily observe both order and disorder. It would not be possible or logical to attribute disorder, evil, to the good soul; it must be assigned to the "contrary" soul. There must be a soul which controls Heaven and earth and which is full of goodness and wisdom. The Supreme Soul must be a perfectly good soul. It must be God. Astronomical evidence cogently testifies that the fundamental movements of the universe are orderly and do not permit of irregularity. No matter how complex the planets may appear to us, their movement is perfectly orderly and mathematically calculable and predictable, so that it is inevitable that we must assert that there is a Supreme Governor behind it all.

Plato now triumphantly concludes his ontological argument with a sweeping statement about the universal cosmos:

> "And certainly shall we not say the same word about all the stars and moon and years and months and all the seasons, that a soul or souls which are noble and possess every excellence have been shown to be causes of all these things? Shall we affirm that they (souls) are gods whether they are in bodies and are living beings and order the entire heaven or wherever and in whatever way they are?"[51]

At this point, before proceeding to the "heresies," it would perhaps be of some value to summarize the points that Plato has brought out in his argument for the existence of God. The first point to be clearly noted is that Plato distinctly attributes evil as well as good to souls. The second point is lucidly apparent, namely, that Plato's God (or gods) is a soul (*psyché*), a supreme *psyché*, to be sure, but nevertheless he is a primary cause, a kínêsis dynaménê autên hautên kineîn. Aristotle's God, the unmoved mover, is an act of perpetual self-contemplation, immanent in himself. Plato's God is teleological: he has a purpose. He is an outgoing projection. He is a creator. The third point is that nowhere is Plato clear on the matter of a God (One God) or gods. To the Greeks this question was not primary. Plato's Supreme Soul is supreme in the hierarchical setup of souls. Plato does not go into details about the lesser souls. The fourth and last point is the fact that Plato's argument is from effect to cause. Plato starts cosmologically with the existence of a world of precise structure. The proof is argument from design.[52]

Plato's next attempt is to crush the "heresies' " very substance. We may sum up the Platonic results here. The atheist will have to disprove the Platonic argument for the existence of God or else be convinced. Plato assumes that the atheist has no alternative but to accept his argument and become a believer. As for the gods' not caring for human matters, Plato asserts that that situation could happen only if we claimed that the gods are incapable of controlling human affairs (which is a blatant absurdity) or because human affairs are too insignificant for divine consideration. Both these claims, Plato postulates, are ridiculous because they are clearly inconsistent with the character of the Supreme Soul. Mortal creatures are "possessions" (Ktêmata) of the gods, just as the "heaven" (ouranós) belongs to the gods. Or to use Plato's medical argument:

> "Consider the case of a physician who is commissioned to cure a certain whole. Consider also that he is willing and able and takes care of the greater parts but neglects the small parts. Will the whole ever be in proper shape?" [53]

Or to use the part and whole argument:

> "And it has not escaped your attention concerning this thing itself that all creation exists for the sake of the whole, in order for the life of the world to be blessed. You are created not for your own sake but for the sake of the whole.

29

For every doctor and every trained craftsman constantly works for the sake of the whole, exerting his efforts towards what in general is best; he works not for the benefit of the part but surely for the sake of the whole."[54]

An interesting feature of the Platonic argument is the attracting pull of the souls. The judgment of the gods is ineluctable:

"This, you see, is the justice (way) of the gods who inhabit Olympus." (Od. XIX. 45)
". . . the worse man goes to the worse souls and the better man to the better and suffers and does what behooves that like should do to like both in (this) life and in every aspect of death. From this justice of the gods neither will you ever succeed in escaping nor any other unfortunate being. The powers who have ordained this justice have decreed that it must be absolutely respected."[55a]

As for the gods' being readily seduced by shrewdly calculated bribe-prayers and sacrifices, Plato asserts dogmatically that such an idea is ridiculous, as if wolves were to give small portions of their ill-gotten prey to watchdogs, and the watchdogs, being placated by such devices, were to participate in this lupine conspiracy, and permit the wolves to continue their wanton attacks on the flocks:

"It is as if wolves were to give small bits of their prey to dogs, and the dogs being pacified by the gifts, were to grant the flocks to them for plunder. Is this not the argument of those who assert that the gods are capable of being appeased by entreaty?[55b]

The gods are "the greatest of all guardians and guardians of the greatest things for us," in Plato's words, and so, with this statement, we may conclude our selection representative of Plato's argument for the existence of God(s).

However, it will remain for the lawgiver to see to it, now that the rationalization of the existence of God has been accomplished, that any disbelievers or misbelievers are appropriately dealt with. The penalties and the offenses are graded; but the magistrates must be very careful to make sure that such cases of "heresy" are brought before the courts for adjudication or else suffer a penalty themselves:

"If anyone commits an act of impiety in words or in deeds, let him who happens to be present act as a defendant by informing the rulers, and let the magistrates who first learn about it bring the man into the appointed court for trial in accordance with the laws. But if the magistrate who has heard the charges does not take action, let him be legally liable to prosecution for impiety by anyone who is willing to render punishment on behalf of the laws. And if a person be convicted, let the court determine the proper penalty for each conviction (act) of impiety."[56]

Plato describes, for the first time in the history of criminological thought, the tripartite division of prisons: (1) common jail for people detained for safe custody in the market place for the majority of cases; (2) a reformatory near to and attached to the Nocturnal Council; (3) a house of correction in the middle of the country, in the wildest and loneliest place possible and suggestive of punishment.[57]

The scheme on page 32 illustrates the breakdown of heretical offenders described by Plato and their designated punishment:[58]

Plato's theology may perhaps be summarized in Plato's own words from the tenth book of the *Laws*:

"It is impossible for any mortal man to become steadfastly god-respecting who does not comprehend these two principles now asserted: namely, that the soul is the oldest of all things that have had a share in generation (i.e. creative activity) and that the soul therefore rules over all bodies. In addition to this, he must comprehend what has up to now often been stated, that the mind controls all things which exist among the stars. . . ."[59]

Man must acknowledge the anteriority of the soul, the immortality of the soul, and the supreme NOUS which governs the universe in order to be considered pious and to insure one's religious happiness. It must be indicated here that Cicero has nothing in his *Laws* even remotely comparable to the scale and importance of the theology of Plato's tenth Book of his *Nómoi*.

Such is our swift survey of religious practices, institutions, theory, and theology as portrayed in the *Laws* of Plato.

TYPE OF OFFENSE	PENALTY
1. Disbelievers in the existence of the gods, but of just character	Admonition and confinement
2. Disbelievers in the existence of the gods, but criminally inclined	Death
3. Believers in divine unconcern with man, but of just character	Admonition and confinement of not less than five years (*Second offense*: Death)
4. Believers in divine unconcern with man, but criminally inclined	Death
5. Believers in the corruptibility of the gods, but of just character	Admonition and confinement. (Upon death loss of burial rights)
6. Believers in the corruptibility of the gods, but criminally inclined	Admonition and confinement. (Upon death loss of burial rights)

IV

Religion in Cicero's *Laws*

Our presentation of religion in Plato's *Laws* probably gave the appearance or impression of disjointedness and isolation. If this is so, it is because the references to religion are woven into the main fabric of the work. To change the figure, the references to religion in the *Laws* are like the individual stones in a mosaic. The removal of even one or two such tesserae is sufficient to distort or destroy the total effect of the picture, or at least to render the picture incomplete. Only in the case of the theology do we get a compact book which we could remove from the work and discuss separately with some safety, but even this constitutes a fundamental book for the whole idea of the *politeia* in the *Laws*. Plato is forceful and in many ways original. He is a profound thinker and arouses many other minds to serious contemplation and action.

When we come to Cicero, we are faced with a completely different situation. Plato's *Laws* are not the Laws of Plato's *Republic*, but Cicero's *Laws* are the Laws of Cicero's *Republic*. Plato's *Laws* is pretty much complete, but Cicero's *De Legibus* is badly mutilated, and we are in no position to state that Cicero ever completed the work. In contrast to the twelve books of Plato's *Laws*, we have three books of Cicero's work by the same name along with a very small fragment preserved from the fifth Book. Unlike our task in the case of Plato, with Cicero our search for references to religion are not scattered throughout the various books, but are clearly and carefully contained in the Second Book, though there are a very few references in

Books I and III. The Second Book of Cicero's *De Legibus* contains the religious laws of Cicero's ideal state. The first Book is introductory; the third deals with a defense of the laws which are primarily concerned with state officials. The three main branches of government—the legislative, the judicial, and the executive—come in for a great deal of attention.

The *De Legibus,* like Plato's *Nómoi,* employs the dialogue. Its effectiveness, it seems to this reader, is undoubtedly greater than in Plato's work. Unlike Plato, Cicero himself takes the chief role (and gives his own name), and Quintus and Atticus are his conversationalists on the long summer day at Cicero's estate at Arpinum. The scene shifts from there to the bank of the Liris and in Books II and III to an island in the Fibrenus. Cicero's Latin is a pleasure to read.

The reader will perhaps find in Cicero's view of religion a tendency to be conservative, traditional, and in accordance with the letter, if not the spirit of Roman religious practice. He should not expect to find any sensational claims by Cicero or any really profound insight into the psychology of religion or major contribution to the philosophy of religion or theology. The reader must at all times remember that Cicero was a Roman, and not a Greek philosopher, no matter how much he espoused the Greek cause. The reader would then perhaps not be surprised to find that Cicero sticks pretty close to the traditional Roman religious "text."

Book I contains two passages which bear upon the discussion of religion in Cicero's *Laws.* They are both concerned with the divine element in mankind. This is a completely different atmosphere from Plato. Unlike anything in the *Laws* that Plato would say, Cicero tries to emphasize the human relationship with God. The soul was generated in us by God, and therefore, there is an *agnatio* between us and the gods, says Cicero. Cicero's argument for the existence of gods (God) is very brief. No creature other than man knows anything of God; among men there is no people either civilized or uncivilized that does not acknowledge the existence of God, though they may not necessarily know particulars about god. So Cicero argues for the existence from universal practice (Plato mentioned this argument,

34

too) and also suggests, in a very Platonic way, that somehow man recognizes God because he recollects the source from which he was created (Compare the Platonic doctrine of recollection). A further argument is adduced from virtue which exists in both man and God, but in no other creature. Virtue, Cicero explains, is nothing more than nature perfected and consummated, "est igitur homini cum deo similitudo." Here are Cicero's words on the preceding:

> . . . quod sparsum in terras atque satum divino auctum sit animorum munere, cumque alia, quibus cohaererent homines, e mortali genere sumpserint, quae fragilia essent et caduca, animum esse ingeneratum a deo. ex quo vere vel agnatio nobis cum caelistibus vel genus vel stirps appellari potest. itaque ex tot generibus nullum est animal praeter hominem, quod habeat notitiam aliquam dei, ipsisque in hominibus nulla gens est neque tam mansueta neque tam fera, quae non, etiamsi ignoret qualem habere deum deceat, tamen habendum sciat. ex quo efficitur illud, ut is agnoscat deum, qui unde ortus sit quasi recordetur et agnoscat.
>
> Iam vero virtus eadem in homine ac deo est neque alio ullo in genere praeterea; est autem virtus nihil aliud nisi perfecta et ad summum perducta natura; est igitur homini cum deo similitudo.[60]

Unlike Plato, Cicero's first remarks that have to do with the argument for the existence of God are succinct and take place comparatively early in his discussion, though they will appear as a point of discussion again later. We may use them as a sort of introduction for our purposes, though this is by no means the way in which Cicero uses them as far as can be determined from the text.

Close to the end of Book I, Cicero points out the divine origin of philosophy and stresses again the divine element in human kind. If only man would realize that he has within an image of God (divinum simulacrum), he would act in the proper way and be worthy of that image. Where Plato stresses the all-embracing universal power of God and the gods, their concern for man's behavior and their incorruptibility, Cicero lowers the stage to the human level. Cicero tries to convince by showing that man is himself divine, so to speak. Therefore, it would not be too much to ask to have one believe in the gods who are man's divine relations *hôs eipein*:

"Ita fit ut mater omnium bonarum rerum sit sapientia, cuius amore Graeco verbo philosophia nomen invenit, qua nihil a dis immortalibus uberius, nihil florentius, nihil praestabilius hominum vitae datum est. haec enim una nos cum ceteras res omnes, tum, quod est difficillimum, docuit, ut nosmet ipsos nosceremus; cuius praecepti tanta vis et tanta sententia est, ut ea non homini cuipiam, sed Delphico deo tribueretur. nam qui se ipse norit, primum aliquid se habere sentiet divinum ingeniumque in se suum sicut simulacrum aliquod dicatum putabit tantoque munere deorum semper dignum aliquid et faciet et sentiet et, cum se ipse perspexerit totumque temptarit, intelleget, quem ad modum a natura subornatus in vitam venerit quantaque instrumenta habeat ad obtinendam adipiscendamque sapientiam. . . ."[61]

We learn further that God is guardian and ruler of heaven and earth, and that the Divine Mind cannot exist without reason, and that it cannot but have the power to establish right and wrong. Law is, in fact, not man-made, but has a divine origin. Law is primal and ultimate—the mind of God "omnia ratione aut cogentis aut vetantis."[62] Therefore, the Divine Mind is the Supreme Law.[63]

Cicero reaffirms the existence of the gods in Book II. He reaffirms what Plato has spent a great deal of text arguing for; namely, the interest of the gods in every individual human being and his religious practices. Like Plato, Cicero points to the astronomical argument for the Divine Existence which Cicero briefly alludes to and which Plato dealt with at length. In other remarks, Cicero becomes very Roman and very practical. Divinity is needed to insure the practical business of oaths, treaties, and the prevention of crime:

"Sit igitur hoc iam a principio persuasum civibus, dominos esse omnium rerum ac moderatores deos, eaque, quae gerantur, eorum geri iudicio ac numine, eosdemque optime de genere hominum mereri et, qualis quisque sit, quid agat, quid in se admittat, qua mente, qua pietate colat religiones, intueri piorumque et impiorum habere rationem; his enim rebus inbutae mentes haud sane abhorrebunt ab utili aut a vera sententia. Quid est enim verius quam neminem esse oportere tam stulte adrogantem, ut in se rationem et mentem putet inesse, in caelo mundoque non putet, aut ut ea, quae vix summa ingenii ratione comprehendantur, nulla ratione moveri putet? quem vero astrorum ordines, quem dierum noctiumque vicissitudines, quem mensum temperatio quemque ea, quae gignuntur nobis ad fruendum, non gratum esse cogunt, hunc hominem omnino numerari qui decet? cumque omnia, quae rationem habent, praestent iis, quae sint rationis expertia, nefasque sit dicere ullam rem praestare naturae omnium rerum, rationem inesse in ea confitendum est. utilis esse autem has opiniones quis neget, cum intellegat, quam multa firmentur iure iurando, quantae saluti sint foederum religiones, quam multos divini suplici metus a scelere revocarit, quamque sancta sit societas civium inter ipsos diis immortalibus interpositis tum iudicibus, tum testibus?"[64]

We now come to the religious laws that Cicero would apply to his ideal state. Cicero would have his laws stated and published in a language not quite as archaic as the Laws of the Twelve Tables and the Sacred Laws, but in order to give them more weight and authority, he would make the language a bit more archaic than the contemporary language. Cicero admits that his laws will be stated concisely with a minimum of detail and gives us the following information: "leges autem a me edentur non perfectae (nam esset infinitum), sed ipsae summae rerum atque sententiae." These laws barely cover three pages in the Loeb text. Their subjects are not unfamiliar to the reader. The text is commonplace. One is almost tempted to say puerile. Cicero is a traditionalist here. He is a conservative. His laws reflect

37

Roman practice. He presents no startling innovations. He presents us with what was hoped to be the practical Roman religious ideal. He also presents us with a deep reverence for ancestral traditions. He has occasional echoes of Platonic influence, but he is essentially a Roman throughout in his religious views. Let us look at the religious laws Cicero proposes and see if we notice anything unusual:

God, the gods, Religious Ritual

1. Ad divos adeunto caste, pietatem adhibento, opes amovento. qui secus faxit, deus ipse vindex erit.

2. Separatim nemo habessit deos neve novos neve advenas nisi publice adscitos; privatim colunto, quos rite a patribus cultos acceperint.

3. In urbibus delubra habento; lucos in agris habento et Larum sedes.

4. Ritus familiae patrumque servanto.

5. Divos et eos, qui caelestes semper habiti, colunto et ollos, quos endo caelo merita locaverint, Herculem, Liberum, Aesculapium, Castorem, Pollucem, Quirinum, ast olla, propter quae datur homini ascensus in caelum, Mentem, Virtutem, Pietatem, Fidem, earumque laudum delubra sunto, nec uncula vitiorum.

The Rites, Holidays, Priests

6. Sacra sollemnia obeunto.

7. Feriis iurgia amovento easque in famulis operibus patratis habento, idque ut ita cadat in annuis anfractibus descriptum esto. certasque bacas sacerdotes publice libanto; hoc certis sacrificiis ac diebus; itemque alios ad dies ubertatem lactis feturaeque servanto; idque ne committi possit, ad eam rem, rationem cursus annuos sacerdotes finiunto; quaeque quoique divo decorae grataeque sint hostiae providento.

8. Divisque aliis alii sacerdotes, omnibus pontifices, singu-

lis flamines sunto, virginesque Vestales in urbe custodiunto
ignem foci publici sempiternum.
9. Quoque haec privatim et publice modo rituque fiant,
discunto ignari a publicis sacerdotibus. eorum autem ge-
nera sunto tria, unum, quod praesit caerimoniis et sacris,
alterum, quod interpretetur fatidicorum et vatium ecfacta
incognita, quorum senatus populusque asciverit; interpretes
autem Iovis optumi maxumi, publici augures, signis et
auspiciis postera vidento, disciplinam tenento; sacerdotes-
que vineta virgateque et salutem populi auguranto,
quique agent rem duelli quique popularem, auspicium
praemonento ollique obtemperanto, divorumque iras providento iisque apparento caelique fulgora regionibus ratis
temperanto, urbemque et agros et templa liberata et effata
habento. quaeque augur iniusta nefasta, vitiosa dira de-
fixerit, inrita infectaque sunto; quique nonparuerit, capital
esto.
10. Foederum pacis belli indotiarum oratorum fetiales iu-
dices nonii sunto; bella disceptanto.

Prodigies and Portents

11. Prodigia portenta ad Etruscos aruspices, si senatus iussit,
deferunto, Etruriaque principis disciplinam doceto. quibus
divis creverint, procuranto, idemque fulgora atque obsti-
ta pianto.

Sacrifices

12. Nocturna mulierum sacrificia ne sunto praeter olla,
quae pro populo rite fient; neve quem initianto nisi, ut ad-
solet, Cereri Graeco sacro.

Sacrilege

13. Sacrum commissum, quod neque expiari poterit, impie
commissum esto; quod expiari poterit, publici sacerdotes
expianto.

Games

14. Loedis publicis quod sine curriculo et sine certatione corporum fiat, popularem laetitiam in cantu et fidibus et tibiis moderanto eamque cum divum honore iungunto.

Ancestral Rites

15. Ex patriis ritibus optuma colunto.

Contributions and Collections

16. Praeter Idaeae matris famulos, eosque iustis diebus, ne quis stipem cogito.

Theft of Sacred Articles

17. Sacrum sacrove commendatum qui clepsit rapsitve parricida esto.

Perjury

18. Periurii poena divina exitium, humana dedecus.

Incest

19. Incestum pontifices supremo supplicio sanciunto.

Bribing the Gods

20. Impius ne audeto placare donis iram deorum.

Vows

21. Caute vota reddunto; poena violati iuris esto.

Consecration

22. Ne quis agrum consecrato. auri, argenti, eboris sacrandi modus esto.

Family Rites

23. Sacra privata perpetua manento.

The Manes

24. Deorum Manium iura sancta sunto, suos leto datos divos habento; sumptum in ollos luctumque minuunto.

The body of Ciceronian religious law is thus swiftly, simply, and briefly executed.[65] It bears a remarkable resemblance to actual Roman practice or at least to what the Romans avowed was their practice. In fact, Cicero admits his lack of originality through the remarks of Quintus: "Conclusa quidem est a te, frater, magna lex sane quam brevi; sed, ut mihi quidem videtur, non multum discrepat ista constitutio religionum a legibus Numae nostrisque moribus." [66] Cicero idealizes the early Roman state. If anything in his proposal seems new, it can be traced back to the practice of the early Romans, and what was best for the early Roman ancestors is certainly best for us, is Cicero's feeling.

The rest of the Second Book is primarily concerned with an expansion of the laws as stated above, mostly in terms of actual Roman practice with occasional citations from Greek examples. Book II of Cicero's *De Legibus* is "an invaluable witness to the conviction, lasting on even in an age of scepticism and indifference among the educated, that the due performance of sacred rites was a necessary function of the State, on which its very existence depended." [67] It will perhaps be profitable to make some observations of the extensive treatment that Cicero makes of his religious laws.

The attitude toward the gods set forth in the first religious law listed above is further clarified. By *caste* Cicero emphasizes the purity of mind, though the purity of body is by no means excluded. Cicero utilizes the Platonic ideal that the *animus* is superior to the body and any blemish of the mind is not eradicable, we are told.

In this same first law, Cicero defines *pietatem adhiberi, opes*

41

amoveri as uprightness that is pleasing to God, but excessiveness is to be avoided. This reflects very much Plato's insistence upon moderation in ritual and funereal matters. Cicero also makes the point that all worshippers are equal in the eyes of God. By *deus ipse vindex* is stressed the fact that no human judge, but God himself is to punish the recalcitrant. Fear of immediate punishment strengthens the power of religion.

Cicero's second religious law forbids the worship of private gods. Plato would be in complete agreement with Cicero on this point, as we have already indicated. Plato would forbid private shrines from being set up. Public worship is encouraged at the public temples under the eyes of the public priests. Cicero doesn't want new or alien gods because they tend to cause confusion to the established religion and because they convey strange ceremonies to the religious scene in which the native priests are not experienced. The best rule to follow in cases like these, Cicero implies, is to trust to our ancestral practices. "Nam a patribus acceptos deas ita placet coli, si huic legi paruerint ipsi patres."

The Ciceronian religious law provides for shrines (*delubra*) in the cities. There is certainly nothing revolutionary in this proposal as it merely reflects both Greek and Roman practice. Cicero interestingly refers to Xerxes who was reported to have burned down the Greek temples (Herod. I, 131; VIII, 109) on the ground that the Greeks confined their gods within walls, whereas the Persians believed that all places consecrated to the gods should be open and free, "quorumque hic mundus omnis templum esset et domus." Cicero counters this Persian argument with the statement that "melius Graii atque nostri, qui ut augurent pietatem in deas, easdem illos urbis quas nos incolere voluerunt." In one of the earliest attempts at comaparative religion, Cicero cites the statement attributed to Pythagoras: "We become best by proceeding to the gods." (Plut: *De Superstitione* 9, 169E) and Thales': "Thales thought that everything is full of gods." (Arist: *De Anima* I, 411A) in support of temples. The power of religion is most deeply felt when we are in the temple (or the modern church), is the argument.

Groves have a similar purpose to that of temples in the country.

A typically Roman emphasis is the importance of the preservation of the rites of the family and the ancestors, which is the provision of the fourth law. This is, of course, in complete agreement with Roman practice. In fact, Cicero adduces the argument that our ancestors were closer to the gods than we are (in point of time, presumably) so that we should respect them all the more.

Souls of all men are immortal, but those of good men are divine, we are informed in Cicero's explanation of the fifth law of his religious series. In this way, it is perfectly legitimate to worship heroes such as Hercules. Cicero also goes into detail to explain that it is a good thing to set up temples and establish worship of good qualities such as those cited by the law, but that temples and worship of vices should be strictly avoided and where actually existing, should be removed. One notices in this Ciceronian proposal the pontifical creations in the old Roman impersonal and daemonic ideas of divine agency or *numen*.

Law number six is self-evident.

Law number seven provides for holidays and is in accordance with actual Roman practice.

Law number eight is again obviously taken from actual practice and the remarks concerned with the Vestal Virgins are traditional Roman concepts and customs.

The ninth law emphasizes that it is important to the state that private worship may not be satisfactorily carried out without those "qui sacris publice praesint." The state is vitally concerned with this matter, since religious advice and authority constitute bonds that hold the state together. Plato would support Cicero in this respect wholeheartedly. Cicero enumerates the priests as follows: (1) those presiding over the regular sacrifices; (2) those who interpret the prophecies of the soothsayers; (3) "maximum autem et praestantissimum in re publica ius est augurum cum auctoritate coniunctum." Cicero, himself an augur, goes on to tell how important this last job really is.

A digression on divination is introduced by Atticus who notes the discrepancies that exist between the two views of two excellent augurs, Marcellus and Appius, one of whom believes that auspices were invented "ad utilitatem esse rei publicae composita, alteri disciplina vestra quasi divinare videatur posse." Cicero puts forth the view that there really is a *mantikē* (observation of birds and other signs—the Roman science of augury), because if we believe that the gods exist, they must give man some indication of things to come. History confirms this, at which point Cicero cites various names and nations. Why even Romulus is indebted to auspices: "nec vero Romulus noster auspicato urbem condidisset." Cicero concludes his argument by stating stoically that: "ita neque illi adsentior, qui hanc scientiam negat umquam in nostro collegio fuisse, neque illi, qui esse etiam nunc putat; quae mihi videtur apud maiores fuisse duplex, ut ad rei publicae tempus non numquam, ad agendi consilium saepissime pertineret."

Law number ten follows Roman practice as does number eleven also.

Law number twelve is in complete harmony with the sentiments of the Roman governmental attitude toward clandestine nocturnal orgies. The classic citation is the Senatorial Decree against the Bacchanalia in 186 B.C. (*C.I.L.* I, 196; Livy XXXIX, 8-20).

Law number thirteen seems self-evident.

Law number fourteen on the games contains nothing worth noting except the Platonic stress on moderation in music to be employed. Cicero discusses Plato's views on music (*Republic* IV 424C-D): "Quam ob rem ille quidem sapientissimus Graeciae vir longeque doctissimus valde hanc labem veretur; negat enim mutari posse musicas leges sine mutatione legum publicarum." Cicero is not so worried or wary. "Ego autem nec tam valde id timendum nec plane contemnendum puto."

Law fifteen repeats law number five with the emphasis on the best. Cicero compares the Athenians' answer from the Pythian Apollo which stated that as for rites "those which were among your ancestors" are to be retained. Again Cicero points out: "et profecto ita est, ut id habendum sit antiquissimum et deo proximum, quod sit optumum."

Law number sixteen reflects Roman practice and number seventeen prescribes no *specific* penalty whereas Plato prescribes death.

44

Laws eighteen and nineteen on perjury and incest respectively require no further comment at this time.

Law number twenty on the wicked attempting to placate the gods with gifts makes the reader refer to Plato (*Laws* IV, 716E). Law number twenty-one on the scrupulous performance of vows brings Cicero into a digression on his own exile. Cicero just cannot help talking about himself even in a discussion of religion:

> "omnia tum perditorum civium scelere discessu meo religionum iura polluta sunt, vexati nostri Lares familiares, in eorum sedibus exaedificatum templum Licentiae, pulsus a delubris is, qui illa servarat. circumspicite celeriter animo (nihil enim attinet quemquam nominari), qui sint rerum exitus consecuti. nos, qui illam custodem urbis omnibus ereptis nostris rebus ac perditis violari ab impiis passi non sumus eamque ex nostra domo in ipsius patris domum detulimus, iudicia senatus, Italiae, gentium denique omnium conservatae patriae consecuti sumus; quo quid accidere potuit homini praeclarius? quorum scelere religiones tum prostratae adflictaeque sunt, partim ex illis distracti ac dissipati iacent, qui vero ex iis et horum scelerum principes fuerant et praeter ceteros in omni religione impii, non solum vita ingnominia cruciati atque dedecore, verum etiam sepultura et iustis exsequiarum caruerunt." (II. 17. 42)

Cicero goes on rhetorically with a tirade against his 'enemies and concludes: "tantum ponam brevi, duplicem ponam esse divinam, quod constet ex vexandis vivorum animis et ea fama mortuorum, ut eorum exitium et iudicio vivorum et gaudio conprobetur."

With regard to law number twenty-two, Cicero translates Plato: *Laws* XII, 955E-956B. In the matter of land, Cicero agrees with Plato, but would not be so strict with respect to the use of gold, silver or ivory for religious purposes.

In explanation of law number twenty-three, Cicero discusses details about hereditary procedures and compares the Scaevolae with the pontifical views. This lengthy discussion tends to be legalistic and will not be discussed here. However, the reader is referred to the work of Dr. Eberhard F. Brück.[68]

The passage that dealt with the Manes (law number twenty-four) has been lost, but a long discussion of graves follows. Various burial methods are dealt with. The Twelve Tables had forbidden burial within the city limits, but exceptions had been made in the case of certain unusual men. No grave is to be permitted in a public place. Funereal expenses are to be moderate. The Twelve Tables are cited for further details on burial customs and procedures. There is no point in citing passages from the Twelve Tables as they merely reflect Cicero's adherence to the traditional Roman customs.[69] Cicero concludes his discussion of religion with Plato (*Laws* XII, 958D-E). Cicero emphasizes Platonic moderation in funeral expenses, but would not himself set exact limits.

"Habetis igitur explicatum omnen, ut arbitror, religionum locum." [70]

This we conclude our lengthy, but by no means exhaustive account of religion in Plato's *Laws* and in Cicero's *Laws*. Perhaps, for Cicero's sake, it would be wise by way of review to cite the excellent summary of Book II of Cicero's *Laws* that Professor A. D. Nock makes in the Cambridge Ancient History:[71]

"Cicero, in the second book of his work *On Laws*, lays down that there are to be no private unrecognized worships: sanction is given only to civic rites in temples or groves and to family rites. Worship is to be directed to the Lares, to the old gods, to those who are recognized as having reached heaven for their merits, and to personified virtues. Emphasis is laid on the maintenance of the priestly colleges and the Vestals, on the augural system (including the observance of the *augurium salutis*), on the control of prophecies (the number must be limited), on the official nature of worship, and on the use of fetials—just as by Augustus. Sacrifices at night are prohibited, with one time-honoured exception (that of Bona Dea): so also initiations except in honour of the Idaean Mother. In the commentary which he then gives he speaks of the nature of purity and of the acceptability of a simple rite, he urges that old temples to evil deities such as Febris should be abolished, and he defends divination by the common custom of humanity."

V

Cicero and Roman Religious Practice

Cicero had declared that compared with other peoples, the Romans were far superior "in religione, id est cultu."[72] He has strengthened his claim in yet another passage where he forcefully asserts: "We have overcome all the nations of the world because we have realized that the world is directed and governed by the will of the gods."[73] *Religio* is a familiar but at times elusive Roman term. It apparently originally had the connotation (in religious terms) of the natural feeling that man manifests in the presence of the supernatural. As a young man Cicero had defined it as the "feeling of the presence of a higher or divine nature which prompts man to worship,—to *cura et caerimonia.*"[74] There is too often the tendency to emphasize the mechanical aspects of Roman religion and to underestimate the religious feelings of the ordinary man. Cicero, like countless others who never had occasion to write a book, supports his native Roman religion against any flagrant foreign influxes. Above, we learned that in his ideal state Cicero would permit no private or foreign gods because "confusionem habet religionum." His own religious setup, his *ius divinum,* Cicero describes as a *constitutio religionum.*[75] The Roman orator elsewhere suggests that *religio* may mean the feeling which suggests worship and the forms under which we carry out that worship. However, we must be careful to distinguish that, although *religio* continues to express the feeling alone or the cult alone, if that is the sense in which it is used, it becomes a more comprehensive term in the time of Cicero because of the philosophic overtones that philosophy has contributed to the word by contemplation of religion as such.

One may perhaps distinguish two aspects of Roman religious practice that are clearly reflected in Cicero's proposed religious laws and which were maintained by the Romans in practice. One is the organizational or civic aspect of Roman religion; the other is the personal, the family or ancestral aspect. W. Warde Fowler has some admirable remarks on the former:[76]

> "In no other ancient State that we know of did the citizen so entirely resign the regulation of all his dealings with the State's gods to the constituted authorities set over him. His obligatory part in the religious ritual of the State was simply *nil*, and all his religious duty on days of religious importance was to abstain from civil business, to make no disturbance. Within the household he used his own simple ritual, the morning prayer, the libation to the household deities at meals; and it is exactly here that we see a *pietas*, a sense of consecrated by religion, which seems to have had a real ethical value, and reminds us of modern piety. But in all his relations with the gods *qua* citizen, he resigned himself to the trained and trusted priesthoods, who knew the secrets of ritual and all that was comprised in the *ius divinum*; and by passive obedience to these authorities he gradually began to deaden the sense of *religio* that was in him. And this tendency was increased by the mere fact of life in a city, which as time went on became more and more the rule; for, as I have pointed out, the round of religious festivals no longer exactly expressed the needs and the work of that agricultural life in which it had its origin."

The Romans were interested in establishing the right relations with the Divine Power or Powers. With their characteristic instinct for order and organization, the Romans set up a permanent authority to take care of the *ius divinum*. Religion became departmentalized. *Pax* with the deities had to be maintained just as diplomatic relations with other powers have to be maintained. Even in the matter of divination, where elsewhere much variety and a certain amount of chaos existed, it is characteristic of the Romans that they systematized the methods employed, especially those that had to do with birds and lightning. This procedure had the result of discrediting a tremendous amount of private activity of this kind. By sanctioning certain religious practices, the State cast a considerable amount of discredit over others that did not have the sanction of the State. This would apply equally to foreign gods as to the possible introduction of new religious institutions.

The other aspect of Roman religion that we might look at briefly is the more closely personal, the more human perhaps, i.e., the family aspect of the Roman's religious life. In the family what rules were needed were, to a great extent, a matter of tradition. The deities involved on the family level were few and the offerings fairly clearly defined. On the state level, a greater deal of know-how was required, a greater organization was needed. Professional priestly colleges had to be formed. There were many diverse deities with diverse desires, inclinations, and functions that always demanded attention. There had had to be a central supervising religious authority to assure the *pax deorum*—an authority which commanded the respect and confidence of all concerned.

The festival of the Lares is a characteristic example of a Roman religious practice at the family level, and one of the religious institutions that Cicero would immortalize in his ideal state. Cicero is a firm believer in the maintenance of ancestral religious practices. The festival of the Lar was celebrated at the *compitum* and hence became generally known as the Compitalia or Laralia. The day of the festival was no doubt set by the paterfamilias in conjunction with other men of his station in the local community or pagus sometime after the winter solstice. The entire family, both free and slave, participated on this cheerful occasion. Each familia performed its sacrifices on its own altar which was situated some fifteen feet in front of the *compitum* in order that the people worshipping might be located in their own property. With the whole pagus (parish) performing this religious ceremony on the same day, there would be a valuable opportunity for a social occasion also. The worshippers could broaden their family perspective in their common religious obligations. This Cicero would describe as the *religio Larium* in Book II of the *Laws* which was "posita in fundi villaeque conspectu," [77] and was an ancient Roman religious tradition.

The personalizing element, the family element, can be seen more humanly in the case of Vesta, the Penates, the Lares, the Genius, the Manes, the numina of the doorway and the spring, all of whom were not to be feared if they were solicitously propitiated. Since the everyday life of the Roman was determined by these divinities, so to speak, by proper propitiation, they could become and did become divine members of the *familia*.

In Tibullus, we find a passage where personal purity is emphasized in the description of a rural festival: [78]

"vos quoque abesse procul iubeo, discedat ab aris
    cui tulit hesterna gaudia nocte Venus.
casta placent superis: pura cum veste venite
    et manibus puris sumite fontis aquam."

The religious purity that the Roman wanted was not merely physical, material purity, but also mental purity. Cicero utilizes the same idea in the *Laws*,[79] though he uses the language of a later age (of Greek philosophy). The personal purity that Cicero would require and that the Roman would require is a survival of ancestral religious tradition. Cicero would, of course, be among the first to defend such an ancestral tradition.

Cicero would then reflect in his *Laws* the best ideals from Roman religious practice. Perhaps, everyone is not observing the ancestral and traditional religious practices as one would like to have them observed, but that would certainly not be a phenomenon confined to Cicero's day. Nevertheless, it would seem that Cicero is giving us a great deal that comes from good old Roman practice and tries to combine the two aspects of Roman religious life, the personal or family one and the civic one into an admirable Roman ideal.

VI

Plato and Cicero: General Conclusions

By way of conclusion, we might repeat that our account was not meant to be exhaustive. We saw briefly two great historical figures interpreting for us their religious views. We found Plato utilizing religion as an important basis for his *politeia* and setting the foundations for natural theology. We saw Cicero leaning on Plato and on the Greeks to a certain extent, but leaning primarily on Roman ideals, on Roman practices, on Roman tradition. Both in Plato and in Cicero, religion is necessary and important for the stability of the state. Plato tends to be very severe in the matter of violations of the established religion; Cicero insists upon the kinship of man with the gods, and implies that the gods could be very useful, in fact have been very useful, if they are properly respected, in the manner of their forefathers. Plato is naturally much more metaphysical and idealistic; Cicero hearkens back to his Roman ancestors and the historical greatness of the Roman state.

VII

The Platonic Attitude Toward Poetry[80]

Plato's attitude toward poetry and the poets in the *Laws* reflects pretty much the same attitude that he held in his earlier *Republic*. However, in Plato's *Laws* his attitude toward poetry and the poets is a consistent one. There are no apparent discrepancies that have to be reconciled nor are there contradictory problems in his attitude that have to be resolved. Though Plato yielded in many details to less stringent measures in his second best *politeía* in the *Laws*, it is noteworthy that his attitude toward the poets become thoroughly crystallized, as fixed and unchangeable as one of his eternal *Ideas*. In his old age, Plato remained as firmly convinced in his unyielding attitude toward the poets as he had ever been, but he does not reject the poets completely nor simply on the grounds that they can never imitate the eternal *Idéai*, but on the contrary, even admits in one place in the *Laws* that the poets are capable of reflecting universal truth.[81] In fact, Plato is perfectly willing to admit the poets into his second-best state, but his utilization of them will be made with extreme caution; his utilization of them will be in strict conformance with poetic standards that the Nomothétês will set up. The poet is recognized and accepted as a powerful educative force and will be admitted to the second best state if he follows the rules of that state and consciously seeks to promote and glorify the rules of that state, particularly the religious and moral rules. These are under no circumstances to be vitiated or unfavorably represented. The gods and their actions are

53

to be pictured in the purest and most brilliant of moral light. Moral education and religion, rightly represented and executed, are absolutely fundamental for the proper functioning of the State and for the stability of the State. Everyone, including the poets, is a part of the State, and must seek to maintain the health, both moral and physical of that which he is a part, and being a part, it is always possible to injure or corrupt the whole with incorrect or heretical ideas.

Though the Platonic attitude toward the poets and poetry forms no major portion of the *Laws* and though no separate book is devoted to the subject, the incidental references scattered throughout this extensive work of Plato's later life are interwoven within the very fabric of the *Laws* and form, so to speak, tesserae of the greater Platonic mosaic. It would appear, upon careful investigation, that the subject of religion together with its closely related theology, form one of the fundamental parts of the Platonic discussion, and it would also appear that the poet, as he has appeared in actuality in the past, has had the dangerous inclination to tamper with the established religious machinery. In fact, it is suggested that the poet has represented views of religion that are absolutely contrary to what religion should be and, according to Plato, what religion really is. The poets have been responsible for disseminating certain immoral representations of the gods and religion and in the *Laws,* there seems to me, there is no more powerful nor bitter Platonic attack than that which Plato maintains against the heretics, among which certainly could be numbered certain poets. Plato very lucidly lists the three types of "heresies." They are as follows: (1) simple atheism: the denial that there are gods of any kind; (2) the doctrine that there are gods, but that they are completely unconcerned with or indifferent to human behavior and humanity; (3) the casual belief that there are gods who render judgment upon man, but that it is possible for the offender to avert divine vengeance by bribing the gods with prayers and sacrifices. This last belief draws up all the venom that Plato can gather. Plato's bitter attack states that it is preferable to believe in no gods at all than hold the belief that gods exist who are not concerned with man and his behavior;

and that it is preferable to believe in gods that are not concerned with human behavior and man than to believe that gods exist and can be bribed or corrupted with special gifts, whatever form they may take. Yet, in the final analysis, Plato would severely punish all three heretical groups and one may say that violators, whether they be poets or just ordinary disbelievers or offenders, are consistently dealt with in Plato's *Laws,* with an iron hand that is not merely iron, but is red-hot iron.

"Plato could become the author of the proposal to 'persecute' for opinions precisely because he held that there are certain beliefs, which are poisonous to the moral life of society, and that these beliefs can be proved to be false." [82]

Book X of Plato's *Laws,* which is practically dedicated in its entirety to the subject of theology contains "the foundation of all subsequent 'natural' theology, the first attempt in the literature of the world to *demonstrate* God's existence and moral government from the known facts of the visible order. First proposal . . . to treat erroneous beliefs about God and the unseen world as crimes, and to erect an inquisition to suppress 'heretical pravity.' At Athens, as in other ancient societies, 'impiety,' that is overt disrespect to the established *cultus* was, of course, a serious offence, but it seems clear that no mere expression about such matters was regarded as criminal." [83]

Plato's great *tour de force* in proving the existence of the gods or God in Book X must also be taken into account. No detailed explanation will be given here but the important stages of the argument will be outlined here inasmuch as this will be the kind of gods (or God) that the poets will have to represent in their religion and, outside of moral education it seems to me it is religion which Plato is saying that the poets should promote with their poetry and it is on religious occasions that the poet would most prominently display his poetic talents. Plato's real arguments for the existence of God begins with the anteriority of the soul. All bodies involve motion or inertia. All bodies are in motion or at rest, used to say the old physics books of our era. Motion or process (kínêsis) is of two types essentially: (1) motion which is capable of moving other things, but not capable of moving itself; (2) motion which is always capable

55

of moving itself and capable also of moving others. The first kind of *kinêsis* may be described as "imparted" or "communicated" motion; the second as "self-originated" motion. Or to use more readily meaningful terms, the second type may be called secondary causation and the first primary causation. Plato goes on to show that primary causation is obviously first, prior both in point of time and quality to all other kinds of motion.

The next step is to show that self-moving motion is indicative of a *psychê*, of somethings *émpsychon*. This step is inevitable. Any object that has the power to move itself as well as other objects contains a *psychê*. Thus we come rapidly to the contention that soul=self-motion or primary causation. Thus our argument is firmly established along with the priority of the soul.

It will therefore follow that the soul is the cause of all things, good and bad, fair and foul, just and unjust, and of all the opposites, if we grant the assumption that the soul is the *Ursache* of all things. Of course, there will have to be more than one soul. In fact, there will have to be at least two souls: a good soul and a contrary or bad soul. There may be as many souls as are needed to explain the actual situation. In the world we can readily observe both order and disorder. It would not be possible or logical to attribute disorder, evil to the good soul; it must be assigned to the "contrary soul." There must be a soul which controls Heaven and earth and which is full of goodness and wisdom. The Supreme soul must be a perfectly good soul. It must be God. Astronomical evidence cogently testifies that the fundamental movements of the universe are orderly and do not permit of irregularity. No matter how complex the planets appear to us, their movement is perfectly orderly and mathematically calculable and predictable so that it is inevitable that we must assert that there is Supreme Governor behind it all. Plato is not clear about the matter of a God (one God) or gods. Plato's Supreme Soul is supreme in the hierarchical setup of souls.[84]

This digression on the Platonic argument for the existence of the gods or god was meant to be suggestive with regard to the poets. The poets must imitate God or gods that are complete goodness and wisdom. Gods can do no wrong. Therefore, it would be very foolish of the poet to represent the god as doing what is contrary to his nature. Nor are the gods unaware or unconcerned with human behavior. Human beings are the ktêmata (possessions) of the gods just as the ouranós (heaven) is. Just as a doctor is concerned with individual treatment of parts of the body for the sake of the health of the whole body, so are the gods concerned for man. Or to use the whole and part argument, man is a part of a greater whole. If the whole is the concern of the gods, certainly the part forms a decided area of interest for the gods.

We could go on with these Platonic arguments but I suspect that it has already been made sufficiently clear how important Book X would be for the poets. The correct representation of the gods and the established religion is vital for the stability of the state and the poets could do nothing better than to contribute their talents to the promotion and maintenance of that stability.

At this point it would perhaps be profitable to look at a number of passages in the *Laws* in which the poets are specifically mentioned, bearing in mind the previous general remarks of Plato about religion. Early in Book II (656C), poets are explicitly denied the right (if such it be) to teach whatever form or rhythm or tune or words that they best like themselves to the children of the law-abiding citizens and young men in the choruses. Plato is interested in preventing the wrong educational and moral result from taking place. He goes on to relate how unfortunately prevalent is the licence afforded poets practically everywhere except in Egypt where music, dance, and poetry have been subjected to rigid moral control with apparently successful moral results: "For it seems that long ago they recognized this principle of which we are now speaking, that the young men of the State should accustom themselves to forms and melodies which are noble: these they determined in detail and set up in the temples, and with the exception of these it was forbidden for painters and all other creative artists to introduce innovations and abandon tradition. This still holds true today whether you consider these arts or the musical art. And if you investigate,

you will find that the things depicted or graven there 10,000
years ago (I do not exaggerate what I say, but literally mean
10,000—ouch hôs épos eipeîn myriostòn all' óntôs) are not a bit
better or worse than the achievements of today but executed
with the same skill. (656C-657A)."
The Egyptian situation aroused Plato's admiration, but one
wonders at the price for the sacrifice. The poets would have to
look to the Egyptian example. Egypt, says Plato, has discovered
the proper tunes and they have been legislated and permanently
consecrated (hóti dynatòn ár'ên perì tôn toioûton nomotheteîs
thai bebaíôs th'hieroûn tà mélê ta tên orthótata phýsei pare-
chómena). This sort of thing must have a divine origin. In
Egypt the goddess Isis is said to have been responsible for the
compositions. Discover the principle of correctness in tune, says
Plato, and reduce it to an incorruptible legal prescription.
The judge of the arts must judge truthfully and not be influenced by the whims of the crowd. We might paraphrase
Plato and say that he wants the critic to criticize freely and fear-
lessly no matter what the majority may feel. "For rightly speaking, the judge sits not as a student, but rather as an instructor
of the spectators, opposing those who give them pleasure in
a way that is unseemly or wrong; just as the present law of
Sicily and Italy now entrusts the decision to the spectators who
determine the winner by show of hands. Not only has it corrupted the poets themselves (diéphtharke mèn toûs poiêtàs
autoús) (for they compose for the cheap pleasure of the judges
with the result that the spectators are themselves the teachers of
the poets), but it has corrupted also the pleasures of the audi-
ence; (pròs gàr tên tôn kritôn hêdonên poioûsin oûsan phaúlên,
hôste autoì autoùs hoi theataì paideúousi) for they should be
constantly improving their standards of pleasure by listening
to those whose characters are better than they, but what they
are now doing happens to be just the opposite."[85]
Plato proceeds with a definition of *paideía* or education.
Education, he says, is the process of drawing and guiding children towards the principle which is pronounced right by the
law and confirmed as truly right by the experience of the oldest
and most just. So it is the duty of the state to see to it that the

right, the desirable system of appropriate stimuli with the appropriate responses is set up in the citizen from childhood.

The same principle applies to the poets. An attempt will be made to train their responses so that they correctly respond to the stimuli with which their poetic talents are confronted. "Similarly the good legislator will persuade the poet by the use of fine praiseworthy words but, if he fails to persuade him, he will compel him to depict by his rhythms the forms, and by his harmonies the melodies of men who are temperate, courageous, and good in all ways. In this way he will compel them to compose their poetry properly." [86]

This Platonic attempt to legislate poetry perhaps strikes strangely upon the modern ear. Yet one may compare a recent measure introduced in the U.S. Congress to legislate on jokes in the entertainment world and protect the jokewriters. Plato would protect the public.

Plato sets down the requirements of a good critic. The critic in order to distinguish between a good poem and a bad poem must know what constitutes tò orthôs. The critic must know the nature of the original; he must know to what extent the copy is correct; and thirdly, the excellence with which the copy has been carried out. [87]

Plato is censuring incongruity, when an artistic piece is disharmonious; lack of meaning, when tunes and gestures have no relationship to words; barbarousness, when the thing represented is mean or insignificant; ostentation, when the person performing renders a performance just to display certain tricks (cf. contortionist). [88]

Book IIIA contains a very important statement about the source of the poet's inspiration and his ability to grasp universal truth. This is preceded by a brief statement earlier (680 B-C) in which Homer is praised and acknowledged as a man of genius ("At least this poet of yours seems to have been accomplished").

Book III tells us that the poet is divinely inspired and is capable of grasping historical truth. "For the race of poets, being divinely inspired in their strains, often comprehends historical truth with the aid of the Graces and Muses." [89] Here Plato clearly recognizes the poet's piercing mind.

59

In Book IV, it is again reiterated that the Nomothétês should not, cannot, permit the poets to compose at will because they might cause injury to the state. Furthermore, very much in the spirit of the *Ion,* Plato refers to the contradictory effect of poetic madness. ". . . Whenever a poet is seated on the Muses' tripod, he is not then in his right mind, but is like a fountain, which allows the current to flow freely; and since his art consists in *mimêsis,* he is compelled to contradict himself, when he creates characters opposed to one another who speak contradictions; and he does not know whether there is any truth in what is spoken or not." [90] Unlike the poet, the lawgiver must always be consistent. There must be no ambiguity about his publications.

Plato takes up the possible damage that the poets could do to religious practices in Book VII (801A) when he defines a prayer (as a request addressed to gods) and warns that poets must not couch bad requests in poetic form with a view toward passing the evil request off as a perfectly good thing. The Platonic penalty for attempting bribery of the gods or even thinking of such a thing is extremely painful. Plato feels the necessity of pointing such matters out because poets (not being completely in control of their senses when composing) are apt to compose contradictory poems, poems that are not in conformance with established practice. The poet must not corrupt the citizen, particularly in the matter of religion.

Again in Book VII (801 D) Plato explicitly informs the poet that he shall compose nothing which the State does not hold to be legal and right, fair and good. Nor will the poet be authorized to show his poems to any private person without first having cleared with the judges and Nomophýlakes. This close control applies to music and songs as well as to poetry. Just think of what Plato could do to modern popular music, movies, and popular literature!

Plato is fully aware of the educative influence and value of the poets and their popularity in his day. However, he is careful to point out though that there are matters in which the poets' utterances would be dangerous to the welfare of the State.

Again a bit later (811B), Plato makes this general concession:

"I think, and in this I suspect everyone will be in agreement with me, that every poet has said a good deal that is good but also a good deal that is just the opposite. If this is really the case, I declare that much learning brings danger to children." [91]

What Plato would like to see embodied in poetic form, what he would consider the sheerest poetry and most suitable for the consumption of the young, are his own philosophical discourses. The Nomophýlax shall be responsible for seeing to it that the teachers teach these philosophical discourses and should he chance upon any poetry or prose or oral compositions that are akin to the Platonic philosophical discourses, it will be his duty to have them set down in writing and promulgated. The teachers must be compelled to learn these, memorize them, teach them and praise them or else be discharged from their positions. [92]

We now come to a very famous, perhaps the most famous passage in the *Laws* as regards Plato's position toward the poets. It is through the mouths of the tragic poets that Plato asks whether the poets are to receive permission for entrance into Plato's second best state: "O, Strangers, are we or are we not to pay visits to your city and country, and traffic in poetry? Or what have you decided to do about this? What would be the right answer to make to these inspired persons regarding the matter? In my judgment, this should be the answer (cf. *Rep.* 398 A,B)—'Most excellent of strangers, we ourselves, to the best of our ability, are the authors of a tragedy at once superlatively fair and good; at least, all our polity is framed as a representation of the fairest and best life, which is in reality, as we assert, the truest tragedy. Thus we are composers of the same thing as yourselves, rivals of yours as artists and actors of the fairest drama, which, as our hope is, true law, and it alone, is by nature competent to complete. Do not imagine, then, that we will ever thus lightly allow you to set up your stage beside us in the marketplace, and give permission to those imported actors of yours, with their dulcet tones and their voices louder than ours, to harangue women and children and the whole populace, and to say not the same things as we say about the same institutions, but on the contrary, things that are, for the most part, just the opposite. In truth, both we ourselves and the whole state would be absolutely mad, were it to allow you to do as I have said, before the magistrates had decided whether or not your compositions are deserving of utterance and suited for publication. So now, ye children and offspring of Muses mild, do ye first display your cants side by side with ours before the rulers; and if your utterances seem to be the same as ours or better, then we will grant you a chorus, but if not, my friends, we can never do so.' "[93]

Hence Plato is explicitly clear about his attitude toward the poets. They must agree to censorship, to supervision if they are to be admitted to the State. Otherwise, they will not be tolerated.

Again in Book VIII (829 D-E), we are informed that no unauthorized song will be permitted "not even should it be sweeter than the hymns of Thamyras or Orpheus—but only such sacred poems as have been approved and have beeen dedicated to the gods or those by good men which have been adjudged to have duly assigned praise or blame." At the religious celebrations those men who are noble and good will be authorized by virtue of the fact that they have rendered noble service to the State to exercise any poetic powers they have. No others are to have this privilege.

So the lawgiver is to be placed far above the poet; for his wisdom is far greater (IX. 858D-859B). Poets have unfortunately been among the numbers of those who have wittingly or unwittingly contributed to the error of disbelief in the gods (and other matters) and have influenced countless others seeking to shun the wrong to do the wrong and attempt to make it appear good (X. 885D). Plato also strikes out against those who have been influenced by the poets in the matter of believing that the gods exist by art and not by nature: the Sophistic view of relativity, that man has created the gods as conventions. This sort of "heresy" Plato just cannot tolerate and the poets have been responsible in that they have succumbed to such malign theories.

As has been sufficiently clearly pointed out, Plato would not exile poetry or the poets from his second best state completely. In fact, he tolerates the poets and recognizes their value to the State if they are willing to submit to censorship, to the proper channeling of their poetic talents for the sake of the State. Plato would admit iambic, lyric, and even comic poetry under the above conditions. However, ridicule of the citizens by word or mimicry, whether with or without passion is strictly forbidden. Any infraction of this rule will subject the violator to a penalty in the form of a fine. Those who have received authorization to indulge in comic poetry may write about each other in jest but without passion. Any violation of this rule will not be tolerated. The Ministry of Education, so to speak, will determine what material can be publicly uttered or published.

The general conclusion drawn is that the lawgiver knows better than the whole tribe of poets what is best for the people (XII. 941 B-C) and consequently he will control the poets. The writings and speeches of the lawgiver (XII. 957D) will serve as the measure of all—poets as well as prose-writers. And so state supervision of poetry recognizes the poet's talents, value, and influence, but fully recognizes that this poetic force may wittingly or unwittingly be wrongly utilized. Therefore, it will be the duty of the Platonic lawgiver to legislate for poetry, to direct poetry and the poets in the proper channels for the good of the State, first by persuasion, and failing that by force. Yet the tacit plea seems to be that the poets will cooperate for the greater benefit of all.

REFERENCES

I

1. Cicero, *De Legibus* I, 15; 20; II, 14; 23; III, 4; 12-13.

II

2. A. du Mesnil in his edition (Leipzig, 1879), pp. 5-6.

3. Plato, *Republic* IX, 592B 2-5.

4. Plato's *Laws* employs three conversationalists, three old men, one of whom is an Athenian, one a Cretan by the name of Clinias, and a third, a Spartan who bears the name Megillus. The Athenian does most of the talking. We might append the epithet *makrológos* to him. His listeners (for such is really the behavioral condition of his companions) have nothing to do and nothing to say that is spectacular or original for the progress of the discussion. Their "national origin" is significant inasmuch as the bulk of the *Laws* for the model *politeia* are in reality drawn from those actually existent in Athens, Sparta, and Crete. The scene is set on the island of Crete, and the discussion occurs during their walk from Knossos to the cave of Zeus on Mount Ida.

5. Plato, *Laws* IV, 714E 6-716B 7. I follow the numbering of E. B. England's edition of the *Laws of Plato* in two volumes, (Manchester: at the University Press, 1921). The reader is referred also to E. R. Dodds: *The Greeks and the Irrational,* (Berkeley and Los Angeles: University of California Press, 1951) for certain relevant remarks on the *Laws* of Plato. The following references to the *Laws* in Dodds may be useful: on the impulses that bring on sacrilege, p. 177 (note 133); discussion on prayer to the sun, p. 232 (note 70); a discussion of the bad soul in Plato's *Laws,* p. 227 (note 24); a discussion concerned with the bribing of the gods, pp. 222-223; on priesthood, p. 233 (note 71).

6. Plato, *Laws* IV, 716B 8-9.

7. Plato, *Laws* IV, 716C 1.

8. Homer, *Odyssey* XVII, 218.

9. Plato, *Laws* IV, 717A 1-718C 3.

10. Cf. Plato, *Laws* X, 910B 8-D 4 below.

11. Plato, *Laws* IV, 717B 6-C 5. This reverence for and attitude toward parents continues unabated even in Modern Greece.

12. Cf. *Matthew* XII, 36.

13. Plato, *Laws* IV, 718A 3-6.

14. A. E. Taylor, *The Laws of Plato* (London, 1934), p. xxxiv.

15. Plato, *Laws* V, 738B 2-E 8.

16. Plato, *Laws* VIII, 848C 7-E 2. Cf. also Ch. Picard: "Les Agoras De Dieux' en Grèce," *British School at Athens Annual,* XLVI (1951), pp. 132-142 on the twelve gods.

17. Plato, *Laws* XII, 955E 4-956B 4.

18. Plato, *Laws,* VI, 771C 6-E 1.

19. Plato, *Laws* X, 909D 7-E 5.

20. Plato, *Laws* X, 910B 8-D 4.

21. Plato, *Laws,* V, 745D 7-E 2.

22. Plato, *Laws* VI, 753B 8-C 4.

23. See note 16 above.

24. Plato, *Laws* VI, 778C 4-D 1.

25. Plato, *Laws* XII, 935A 6-B 5. Cf. A. D. Nock: "Cult of Heroes," *Harvard Theological Review,* XXXVII (1944), pp. 141-174.

26. Plato, *Laws* XII, 950E 4-951A 2.

27. Plato, *Laws* VI, 759A1-760A 5. On the *exêgetai,* cf. the articles by James H. Oliver and Herbert Bloch on the subject. Herbert Bloch: "The Exegetes of Athens and the Prytaneion Decree," *American Journal of Philology,* LXXIV (1953), pp. 407-418. Oliver bitterly criticizes both Bloch's views and Bloch's methods in his article, James H. Oliver: "Jacoby's Treatment of the Exegetes," *A. J. P.,* LXXV (1954), pp. 160-174. Oliver contends that Jacoby's and Bloch's views on the number of exegetes and on the history of the institution are ill-founded; he further asserts that Bloch's article is not the critical independent article that it purports to be. Cf. also Bloch's latest reply, "The Exegetes of Athens: A Reply," *Harvard Studies in Classical Philology* LXII (1957), pp. 37-49.

28. Plato, *Laws* VIII, 828A 1-D 5.

29. Plato, *Laws* VIII, 829B 7-C 5.

30. Plato, *Laws* II, 653C 9-D 5.

31. Plato, *Laws* VII, 799A 4-B 8; p. 82 of A. E. Taylor's translation. Cf. also W. C. Greene: "Plato's View of Poetry," *Harvard Studies in Classical Philology* 29 (1918), pp. 1-75. On Moira cf. William Chase Greene, *Moira* (Cambridge Mass.; Harvard University Press, 1944).

32. Plato, *Laws* VII, 801A 8-B 3.

33. Plato, *Laws* VII, 801E 1-4.

34. Plato, *Laws* XII, 958E 6-959A 4.

35. Plato, *Laws* XII, 947A 4-E 5.

36. Plato, *Laws* XII, 951D 7-E 3.

37. Plato, *Laws* IX, 853-854.

III

38. A. E. Taylor, *The Laws of Plato,* p. li.

39. A. E. Taylor, *The Laws of Plato,* p. li.

40. Plato, *Laws* XI, 930E 7-931A 3.

41. Plato, *Laws* X, 886A 1-5.

42. Plato, *Laws* X, 886D 4-E 2. Cf. Taylor's introduction to the *Laws*, p. liii.

43. Plato, *Laws* X, 888C 1-C 7.

44. Plato, *Laws* X, 893B-899B.

45. Plato actually lists ten kinds of motion: (1) circular motion round a fixed center; (2) locomotion; (3) combination; (4) separation; (5) increase; (6) decrease; (7) becoming; (8) perishing; (9) secondary causation; (10) primary causation. The last two are the ones that are really significant for any discussion. On Platonic motion and the soul consult Harold Cherniss's review of A. J. Festugière: "La Révélation d'Hermès Trismégiste II, Le Dieu Cosmique," in *Gnomon,* 1950, pp. 204-16, but especially pp. 207-210. On motion in the *Timaeus* and the *Laws* and the World Soul, consult M. Meldrum: "Plato and the Ἀρχὴ Κακῶν," *Journal of Hellenic Studies* LXX (1950) pp. 65-74.

46. Plato, *Laws* X, 895D 4-5.

47. Plato, *Laws* X, 896A 1-2.

48. Plato, *Laws* X, 896A 3-4

49. Cf. Plato, *Phaedrus* 245C-E.

50. Plato, *Laws* X, 896E 5-6. Cf. H. Cherniss on the soul as cited above, note 45.

51. Plato, *Laws* X, 899B 3-10.
52. See pp. liv-lv of A. E. Taylor's *The Laws of Plato.*
53. Plato, *Laws* X, 902D 2-5.
54. Plato, *Laws* X, 903C 2-D 1.
55ª. Plato, *Laws* X, 904E 4-905A 4.
55ᵇ. Plato, *Laws* X, 906D 2-5.
56. Plato, *Laws* X, 907D 7-E 7.
57. Plato, *Laws* X, 908A 1-7.
58. Plato, *Laws* X, 908A-909D 1.
59. Plato, *Laws* XII, 967D 4-E1.

IV

60. Cicero, *De Legibus* I, 7. 24-25.
61. Cicero, *De Legibus* I, 22. 58-59.
62. Cicero, *De Legibus* II, 4. 8.
63. Cicero, *De Legibus* II, 4. 11.
64. Cicero, *De Legibus* II, 7. 15-16.
65. Cicero, *De Legibus* II, 8. 19-9. 22.
66. Cicero, *De Legibus* II, 10. 23.
67. W. Warde Fowler, *The Roman Festivals of the Period of the Republic* (London, 1899), p. 333.
68. Cicero, *De Legibus* II, 10. 24-21.53 includes Cicero's explanations of his religious laws. The method of noting every passage has been abandoned at this point as being too clumsy since the discussion follows the text in order. Cf. E. F. Bruck, "Cicero vs the Scaevolas, re: Law of Inheritance and Decay of Roman Religion," *Seminar* III (1945), pp. 1-20.
69. Cicero, *De Legibus* II, 21. 54-26. 66.
70. Cicero, *De Legibus* II, 26. 69.
71. A. D. Nock in the *Cambridge Ancient History* X (1934), pp. 469-470. Cf. also the chapters on Roman religion in *C. A. H.* X (1934), pp. 465-511; VIII (1930), pp. 423-464; XII (1939), pp. 409-449.

V

72. Cicero, *De Natura Deorum* II, 8.
73. Cicero, *Harusp. resp.* 19.
74. Cicero, *De Inventione* II, 161.

75. Cicero, *De Legibus* II, 10. 23.

76. W. Warde Fowler, *The Religious Experience of the Roman People* (London, 1911), pp. 226-227.

77. Cicero, *De Legibus* II, 19 & 27.

78. Tibullus II, I. 11.

79. Cicero, *De Legibus* II, 10. 24-25.

VII

80. This supplementary chapter, which may be read as an independent essay, has been added in the belief that Plato's attitude toward the poets is intimately connected with the basic religious and theological principles set up by Plato in the *Laws*. The reader is again referred to W. C. Greene, "Plato's View of Poetry," *H. S. C. P.* 29 (1918), pp. 1-75. Cf. also Constantine Vourveris, "Παιδιὰ καὶ Παιδεία (Σωκράτης-Πλάτων-'Αριστοτέλης)" in 'Επιστημονικὴ 'Επετηρὶς τῆς φιλοσοφικῆς Σχολῆς τοῦ Πανεπίστημίου 'Αθηνων VI (New Series), (1955-56), pp. 469-526.

81. Plato, *Laws* III, 682A, where Plato credits the poets with often being able to grasp universal (historical) truth with the aid of the Muses and Graces because they are a divinely inspired group.

82. Cf. note 38.

83. Cf. note 39.

84. Cf. note 24-26.

85. Plato, *Laws* II, 659A-E.

86. Plato, *Laws* II, 660A.

87. Plato, *Laws* II, 668C-D.

88. Plato, *Laws* II, 669C-E.

89. Plato, *Laws* III, 682A.

90. Plato, *Laws* IV, 719C-D.

91. Plato, *Laws* VII, 811B.

92. Plato, *Laws* VII, 811C-E, 812 A.

93. Plato, *Laws* VII. 817A-D. Loeb Library translation. R. G. Bury, *Plato with an English Translation IX Laws in Two Volumes,* Vol. II (Cambridge, Mass. 1952), p. 99. Quoted with the permission of the Harvard University Press.

GENERAL INDEX